The Anchor of Our Purest Thoughts (Book 5)

STRATEGIC MEMORY

The Natural History of Learning and Forgetting

DR. CHONG CHEN

Brain & Life Publishing
London

Copyright © 2018 by Chong Chen, PhD

All Rights Reserved. No reproduction of any part of this book may take place without the written permission of the publisher, except in the case of brief quotations embodied in book reviews and other educational and research uses permitted by copyright law.

ISBN 9781912533046 Paperback

Brain & Life Publishing

27 Old Gloucester Street, London, U.K.

First Printing, May 2018

For information about special needs for bulk purchases, sales promotions, and educational needs, please contact orders@brainandlife.net.

The Anchor of Our Purest Thoughts Series

1. *Fitness Powered Brains: Optimize Your Productivity, Leadership and Performance*

2. *Chocolate and the Nobel Prize: The Book of Brain Food*

3. *Cleverland: The Science of How Nature Nurtures*

4. *The Tale of Two Minds: The Art and Science of Decision-making in Everyday Life*

5. *Strategic Memory: The Natural History of Learning and Forgetting*

To Arisa and my parents for their love and support

Memory is the treasury and guardian of all things.

— Cicero

Table of Contents

Preface 1

Part 1: The Process of Memory 5

  Chapter 1: Over a Century of the Forgetting Curve 6

  Chapter 2: Forgetting Curve after Rote Learning 17

  Chapter 3: Ebbinghaus' Concern: What Is the Use of Sleep? 23

  Chapter 4: Research Advances on the Process of Memory 30

  Chapter 5: Revisiting Sleep 39

Part 2: The Encoding and Storage of Memory 49

  Chapter 6: Things Are Better Remembered When We Pay Attention 50

  Chapter 7: Multiple Modes of Encoding 58

  Chapter 8: The Modality Effect and Multimedia Learning 63

Part 3: Schema and Systems Consolidation 69

  Chapter 9: How Prior Knowledge Changes Learning 70

  Chapter 10: Schemas 77

  Chapter 11: Meaningful Learning 84

  Chapter 12: Elaborative Encoding That Promotes Systems Consolidation 90

Part 4: Memory Retrieval and Reconsolidation 97

    Chapter 13: The Testing Effect..98

    Chapter 14: Memory Retrieval Is a Cue-guided
                      Search Process 108

    Chapter 15: The Context of Memory..............................114

    Chapter 16: Spaced Learning..121

    Chapter 17: Interleaved Learning 130

    Chapter 18: What Causes Forgetting:
                      Memory Interference 135

    Chapter 19: Memory Retrieval Is a Reconstruction
                      Process: The Side Effect of Schemas.........143

Part 5: Mnemonics...151

    Chapter 20: How Do Mental Athletes Remember
                      Everything?..152

    Chapter 21: Visual Imagery..156

    Chapter 22: The Method of Loci 164

    Chapter 23: The Peg-Word System 170

Conclusions..173

References...175

Index 197

About The Author 201

Preface

Ask any psychologist and they will say, ultimately, we are our memory. Ask any neuroscientist and they will say we are our synapses. In another book on brain food, I wrote, "…we are what we eat." There is a common theme behind these statements and that is how our brain works.

Memory is stored in the synapses that connect neurons. All our experiences including thoughts and feelings are built upon the synapses and contained in our memory. What we eat changes the neurobiology of our neurons and memories.

The ability to memorize is of crucial importance. Memory and intelligence go hand in hand. Those that are smart remember things faster and more accurately. Those with a strong memory are often good at reasoning and making decisions. Meanwhile, decades of research suggest that the expertise of many professionals is deductible to their memory of a large number of patterns and chunks.

Even if you don't have a good memory, the good news is, we can improve our memory and expertise, by means of learning. The key, therefore, is located in what kind of learning is most effective and efficient.

Rote learning is inefficient, for instance, as it is not optimal to learn things solely by repeatedly studying them. Everyone knows this yet, many still use it. Have our schools and families forgotten, or perhaps, don't know how to teach us more effective and efficient strategies.

Partly because of our longing for superior memory and partly due to media influence, memory champions are getting a greater audience. It has become clear that the memory champions have no super memory and what makes them good at remembering random, nonsense information is the mnemonics they use.

Typical examples of mnemonics are the method of loci and the major system (see Part 5). In the method of loci, you associate new information with familiar places in your "mind palace." When you recall the information, you walk through those places and collect the information. In the major system, you convert numbers to words and then form meaningful stories. Using the major system and the method of loci, when I was at graduate school, I remembered the first 1,100 digits of pi in a week by linking the converted words to shops and restaurants on my way to school.

The excitation of the "strategic, superior memory," however, only lasted a few weeks. I soon found that despite being helpful in remembering digits, names, and cards, the mnemonics hardly assisted in my general learning. They are not beneficial to our learning of knowledge at work and school. Nor do they bring insights or enhance creativity.

Therefore, I looked at the scientific study of memory and learning. As a neuroscientist, the questions I asked over the past years were "How much knowledge have humans gained regarding the 'natural history' of memory? How is a memory created, stored, and forgotten in the brain? How can we recall a specific piece of memory? What are the effective and efficient strategies to memorize things?"

This book is an answer to these questions. Here I introduce state-of-the-art scientific knowledge on memory and show you the data of many groundbreaking studies conducted in the past roughly one and a half centuries. Through looking at the "law" of memory, we will get familiar with the available strategies towards superior memory.

PART 1
The Process of Memory

Chapter 1
Over a Century of the Forgetting Curve

Since the scientific revolution, observation and experiment have become the golden standard for obtaining truth. Two decades after Charles Darwin and Alfred Russel Wallace put forward the theory of evolution by natural selection, in 1879, Hermann Ebbinghaus, a 29-year-old German philosopher, began to study memory in a scientific way.

The young Ebbinghaus started his seven-year European trip after earning a doctorate in 1873. Although the topic of his dissertation was subconsciousness, he was more interested in history and philosophy.

During his travel, at a second-hand bookstore in Paris, Ebbinghaus came across a book written by German philosopher, physicist, and experimental psychologist Gustav Theodor Fechner, *Elemente der Psychophysik [Elements of Psychophysics]*. In this book, Fechner argued that the mind and the body are two sides of the same reality and the mind could be measured by perception and sensation. Fechner further developed experimental methods for measuring sensations, which marked the birth of a new discipline: psychophysics.

Ebbinghaus immediately became fascinated with memory and this empirical approach. He decided to use it to study memory. Prior to that, studying memory was philosophers' work. Philosophers came up with various explanations about memory and disputed about those explanations with each other, all without collecting any convincing evidence. Ebbinghaus was the first to use objective experiments to study the mysteries of memory.

Forgetting curve of a brief learning

To simplify the problem, Ebbinghaus invented nonsense syllables. Nonsense syllables are consonant-vowel-consonant combinations such as DAX, HIW, BIJ, and LEQ. These syllables are pronounceable but contain no meaning. Ebbinghaus thought by using these as the material, he could study pure memory (i.e., learning and forgetting) without the interference of the word meaning. He started experiments with himself as the subject.

Under strict laboratory conditions, Ebbinghaus forced himself to recite a large number of nonsense syllables and recorded how many times and how much time he needed to remember them. He then tested his memory at the same time every day. The metric he used was how many additional times it took him to memorize the syllables. The more times of extra repetitions required for learning, the more forgetting occurred to the original memory. In this way, Ebbinghaus finally discovered the groundbreaking "forgetting curve."

As can be seen from Figure 1.1, the sharpest decline in memory occurs in the first 20 minutes after learning: over 40% of the original remembered information is lost. The speed of forgetting is fast, and the decay is substantial throughout the first day, during which period over 65% is forgotten.

After the first two days, forgetting becomes slower: 6 and 31 days after learning, about 75% and 80% is forgotten.

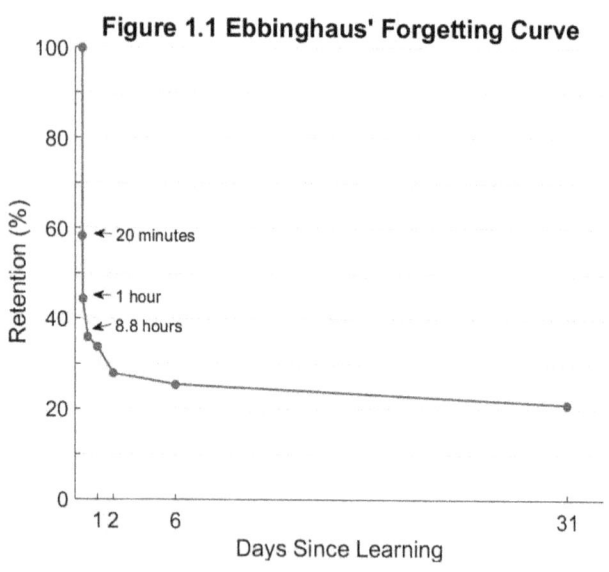

The nonsense syllables used by Ebbinghaus have been criticized by later psychologists for being meaningless and irrelevant to our learning in everyday life. The criterion used by Ebbinghaus to evaluate memory and learning—how many additional times or how much additional time it takes to memorize the information again—is not practical and has been abandoned.

Nevertheless, the shape of the forgetting curve discovered by Ebbinghaus proves to be a core trait of human memory.

<u>With the passage of time, memory decays. The decay is fast at first, particularly in the first few days, after which it gradually levels off.</u>

The forgetting curve has been confirmed using meaningful materials such as words, personal events, and professional knowledge, and with different tests.

In 1929, W. C. F. Krueger at the University of Chicago reported the forgetting curve of word lists. Krueger asked people to memorize several lists of monosyllable nouns by heart and later asked them to recall those words without giving them any cues.

As shown in Figure 1.2, 1 day after learning, about 75% of the words are forgotten; 4 days later, 95% has been lost from memory; 28 days later, people recall none of the words.

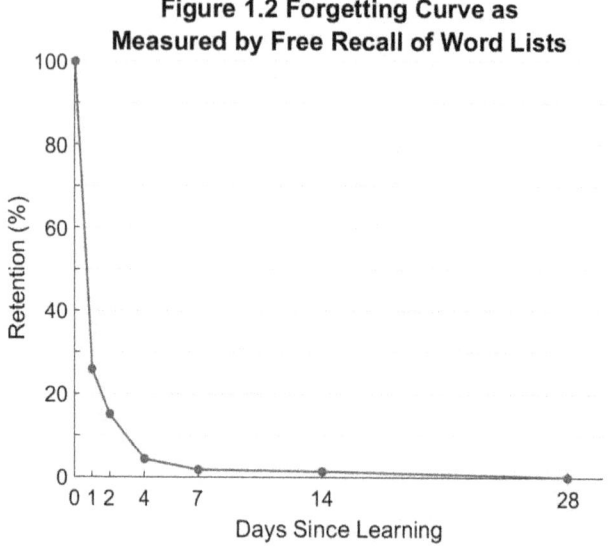

Figure 1.2 Forgetting Curve as Measured by Free Recall of Word Lists

The irrelevant words on the lists are not easily remembered. In free recall tests, people must rely on their own memory and no external cues to recall the information. As we will see later, free recalling with no cues is hard, because memory retrieval is a cue-guided search process (Chapter 14).

In contrast, meaningful, important information, such as people's life events, is more memorable. In 1982, Charles P. Thompson at Kansas State University asked college students to make notes of two unique events that happened to two of their roommates each day. Unique was defined as typically occurring no more than once in a semester. Examples are a breakup with one's romantic partner, and being elected to a special position.

Later, research assistants read each event to the two roommates and asked them to estimate the date on which it occurred. Their forgetting curve is shown below.

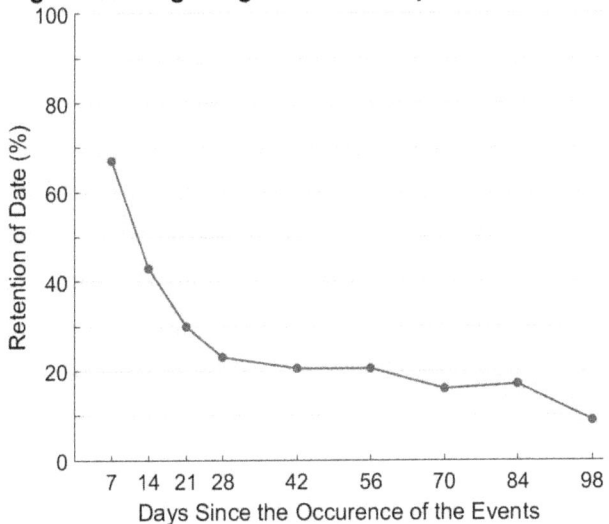

Figure 1.3 Forgetting Curve of Unique Personal Events

Comparing this forgetting curve with the previous one of word lists, we will find that the decay of unique personal events is slower: 7 and 28 days later, over 65% and 20% can still be recalled.

Compared to meaningless information, meaningful information is remembered better and its decay is slower.

As we will see later, meaningful information is encoded at a deeper level and more reliably stored in long-term memory (Chapter 6).

The forgetting curve also applies to learning that persists for a longer period, for instance, the knowledge we learned at high school and in college.

Forgetting curve of high school and college knowledge

Martin A. Conway at Lancaster University, U.K., studied the long-term retention of the concepts of cognitive psychology in students enrolled in a college psychology course. The concepts included memory, perception, language, problem-solving, research methods, and artificial intelligence.

Conway differentiated two forms of memory, recognition, and recall. In the recognition test, students had to indicate whether a particular item had appeared in their courses during college. In the recall test, certain names or concepts were deleted from a list of statements and the students had to fill in the "blanks." The results of their retention are shown in Figure 1.4.

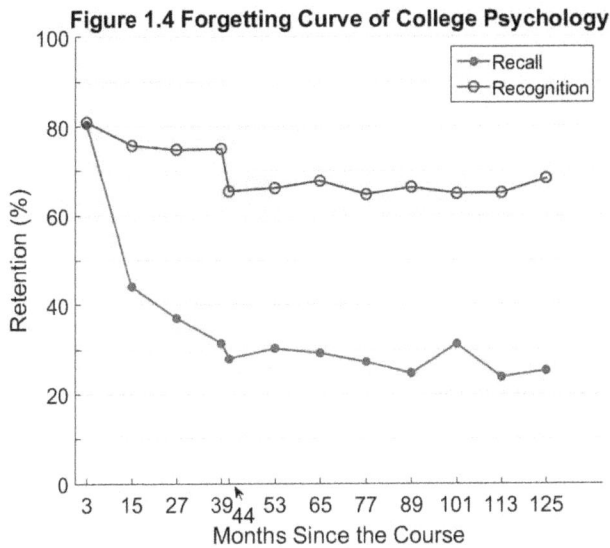

Figure 1.4 Forgetting Curve of College Psychology

The forgetting curve of recall resembles a typical forgetting curve that shows memory decays with the passage of time. However, this is not the case with recognition, which only shows a slight decline. We have recognition memory of things as long as we remember learning about them even if we cannot recall them, or we don't remember the specific details. Over 10 years later, the retention rate on tests of recognition is still as high as almost 70%.

This trend is again confirmed by another long-term study. Harry P. Bahrick at Ohio State University studied American people's memory of Spanish learned in high school and college and repeatedly tested them during the following 50 years.

He also differentiated recognition from recall. In the recognition test, people were presented Spanish words and had to select the corresponding English words from several options. In the recall test, they were presented Spanish words and had to recall the corresponding English words. The results are shown in Figure 1.5.

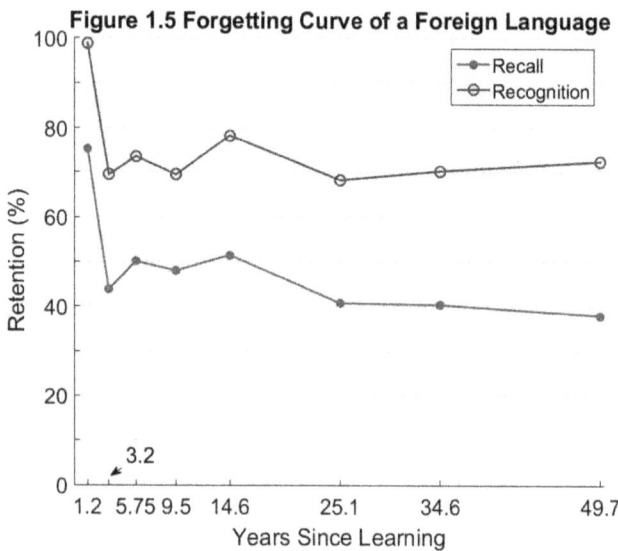

The most forgetting of knowledge learned at school appears in the first 3 years, after which the decay becomes minimal.

50 years after the initial learning, the recognition memory is still over 70% accurate, while the recall memory is about 40% accurate. Some memory, when not recalled, can still be recognized. It is because, during recognition, a cue is provided which guides retrieval.

<u>Recognition memory is better than recall memory.</u>

In this study, Bahrick further adjusted the performance of the subjects according to their original scores achieved in school. Strikingly, those with higher scores in school had a slower decay of memory. The result from the recognition test is shown in Figure 1.6.

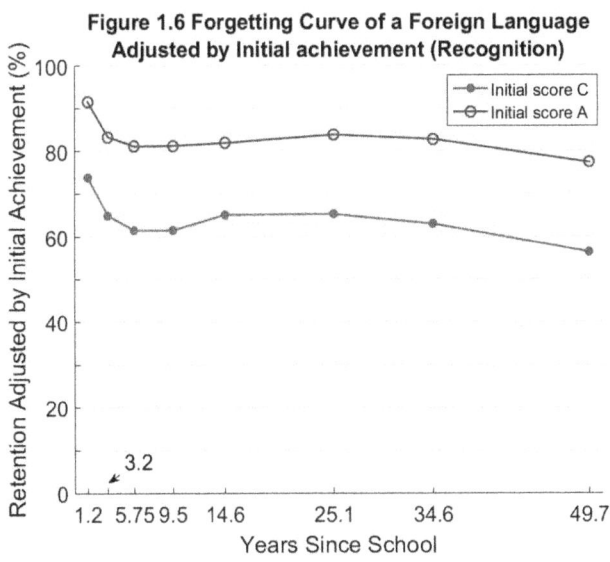

<u>Those who initially learn better will forget what they have learned at a slower rate.</u>

There seems to be two explanations for this phenomenon. First, those who achieve higher scores in school had greater memory ability and could remember what they learned better. Second, regardless of memory ability, people who learn something better (deeper or more systematic) forget what they have learned slower. The first explanation is common sense. The second is supported by the theory and observation on deep processing; that is, information processed at a deeper level will be retained better (see Chapter 6).

Chapter 2
Forgetting Curve after Rote Learning

The second discovery made by Ebbinghaus was repetition enhances memory. In his experiment, on the first day, Ebbinghaus randomly chose a series of new, nonsense syllables. He recited them for 8, 16, 24, 32, 42, 53, or 64 times. The next day, Ebbinghaus recited these syllables again and recorded how much additional time he needed to remember them. Figure 2.1 is the result he found.

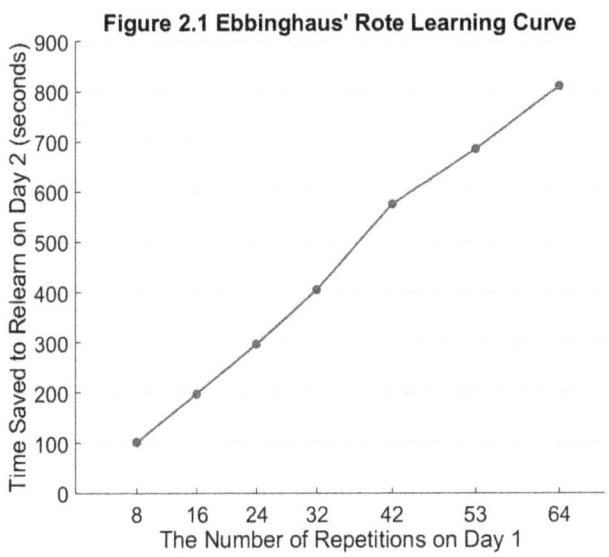

Figure 2.1 Ebbinghaus' Rote Learning Curve

The more times spent learning the same material, the less time to relearn it and the more time saved.

<u>The amount learned depends on the time spent learning. The longer time you learn something, that is, the more times you repeatedly recite something, the better you can memorize it.</u>

This is known as the *Total Time Hypothesis*. It is consistent with the general rule of "no pain, no gain" and "you get what you pay for." Essentially, this is rote learning: the memorization of information is based on pure repetition.

This phenomenon is subsequently studied under the paradigm "overlearning." 100% learning refers to the minimum amount of learning required to memorize the information initially. Say we must recite a word list 10 times to remember it. Overlearning, for example, 150% learning, means we increase the times of learning by 50%. Instead of reciting the word list 10 times, we recite it 15 times. Similarly, 200% learning means we double the amount of learning, which in this case would be 20 times.

In the 1929 study we mentioned earlier, W. C. F. Krueger asked people to learn a series of monosyllable lists of nouns and discovered this forgetting curve shown in Figure 2.2.

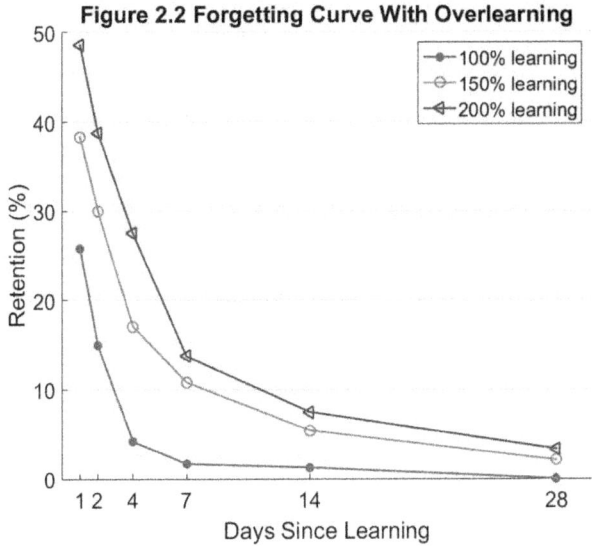

Figure 2.2 Forgetting Curve With Overlearning

Overlearning enhances memory and reduces forgetting. But as can be seen, the improvement of memory from 150% to 200% learning is smaller compared to that from 100% to 150% learning. It suggests that, as the degree of overlearning increases, the improvement in learning decreases.

Meanwhile, as time passes, the memory-enhancing effect of overlearning becomes smaller: 28 days after learning, the benefits of overlearning becomes minimal.

<u>Rote learning is of low efficiency. The same amount of effort does not always bring the same amount of gain. In the long run, the benefit of rote learning is negligible.</u>

This has been validated by many later studies. In 1992, James E. Driskell at Rollins College, U.S., conducted a meta-analysis of 88 studies on overlearning and confirmed that overlearning enhances memory. However, whereas more overlearning is associated with a bigger memory-enhancing effect, the same degree of overlearning does not always bring the same degree of memory benefits. As the degree of overlearning increases, the improvement in memory progressively decreases. This is shown in Figure 2.3.

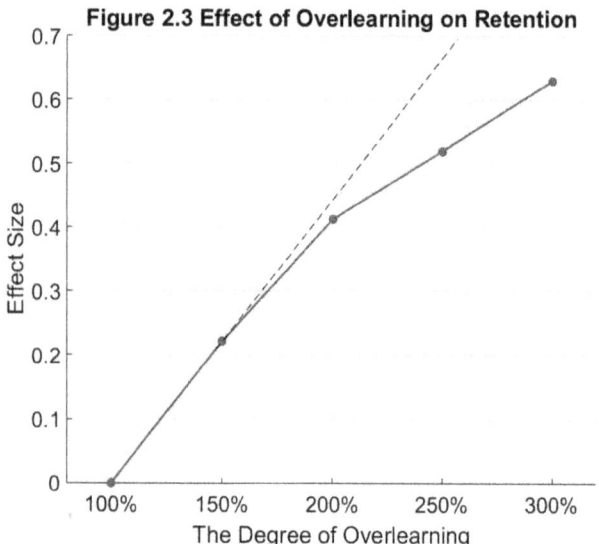

Furthermore, as the time interval between learning and testing increases, the effect size of overlearning decreases, as shown in Figure 2.4. 38 days after learning, the effect size becomes 0.

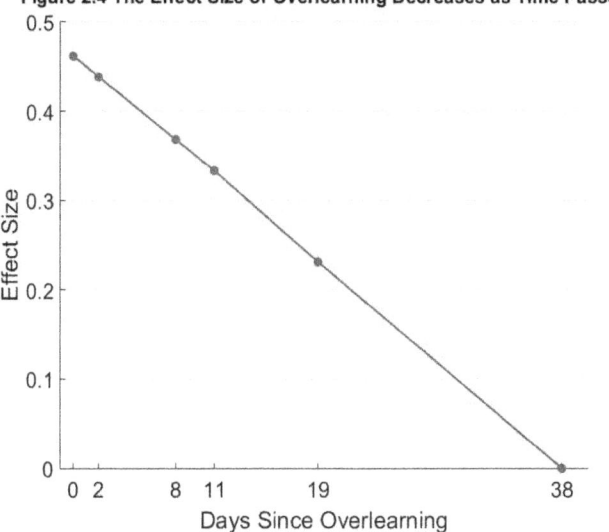

Figure 2.4 The Effect Size of Overlearning Decreases as Time Passes

The poor efficiency of overlearning is well illustrated by a 2005 study conducted by Doug Rohrer at the University of South Florida. Rohrer asked subjects to learn the definition of a series of new words. Those in the general learning group studied a list of 20 words for 5 sessions, while those in the overlearning group studied a list of 10 words for 10 sessions.

Obviously, the overlearning group would remember the definition of the words better. As predicted, 87% subjects in the overlearning group got 100% right at least three times on later tests. For the general learning group, 98% never exceeded one time of 100% right.

However, as time passed, the benefit of overlearning reduced. When tested 4 weeks later, those in the general learning group who studied 20 words for 5 sessions could correctly recall the definition of 3.7 words. In contrast, those in the overlearning group who studied 10 words for 10 sessions could only recall 2.2 words.

As we can see, the efficiency of overlearning is rather low. As there are many more effective and efficient learning strategies, overlearning or rote learning is not recommended.

CHAPTER 3
Ebbinghaus' Concern: What Is the Use of Sleep?

What could not be repeated at first is readily put together on the following day; and the very time which is generally thought to cause forgetfulness is found to strengthen the memory.

Quintilian, *Institutio Oratoria [Institutes of Oratory]* (First Century AD)

If we look at Figure 1.1 again, we see that the forgetting curve is not a beautiful, natural one: the data point at day 1 is an outlier. Ebbinghaus noticed this, too.

Ebbinghaus thought that the three data point at 8.8-hours, day 1, and day 2 were the most unsatisfactory because they were not harmonious with other data. During the 15-hour period from 8.8-hours to day 1, the increasing in forgetting was 2.1%. In contrast, during the 24-hour period from day 1 to day 2, the increasing in forgetting was 5.9%. Unproportional.

"Such a relationship is unbelievable because, based on all other data, as time passes, here forgotten significantly delayed," argued Ebbinghaus.

In 1924, psychologists John G. Jenkins and Karl M. Dallenbach investigated this phenomenon. They used Ebbinghaus' nonsense syllables as material for their two subjects.

The two subjects learned 6–7 lists of 10 nonsense syllables, some during the daytime (8:00–10:00 am), some during the nighttime (11:00 pm–1:00 am). After each daytime study, they stayed awake as usual. After each nighttime study, they slept as usual. The researchers tested their memory of the syllables for the following 8 hours. For the nighttime study, they were woken up and tested at specific times. The result is shown in Figure 3.1.

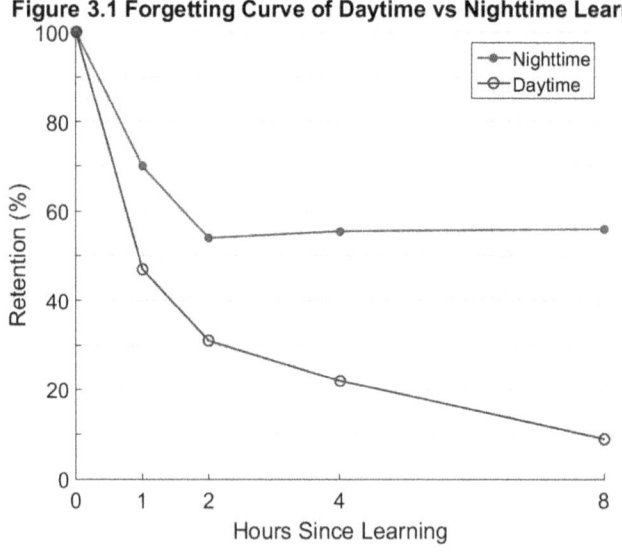

Ebbinghaus' Concern: What Is the Use of Sleep?

During nighttime, forgetting increased to 2 hours after learning, after which it became minimal: memory became stabilized. In contrast, during daytime, forgetting continued to increase until 8 hours later since learning. Forgetting during daytime was substantially faster compared to that during nighttime.

<u>Compared to in the morning, learning at nighttime results in better memory.</u>

The researchers thought that during sleep, people have less interference from other factors; therefore, their forgetting is lower compared to during wakefulness. This is one explanation (see Chapter 18). Later research discovered another more important explanation: sleep itself is important to the consolidation of memory something we will introduce in-depth soon. For here, we give two more examples.

A subsequent 1972 study conducted by British psychologists at the University of Durham looked at the effect of learning in the morning versus evening, and before sleeping versus wakefulness. They had four groups of subjects learn a list of 30 two-syllable nouns and tested them immediately and 5 hours after learning. Both test used free recall (without cues).

The Morning-Wake group learned in the morning at 6:30 am and stayed awake after that, engaging in their usual activities such as reading, shopping, or taking classes.

The Morning-Sleep group learned in the morning and slept after that.

The Night-Wake group learned in the evening at 11:00 pm and stayed awake after that.

The Night-Sleep group learned in the evening and slept after that.

The performance of the subjects in these four groups is shown in Figure 3.2.

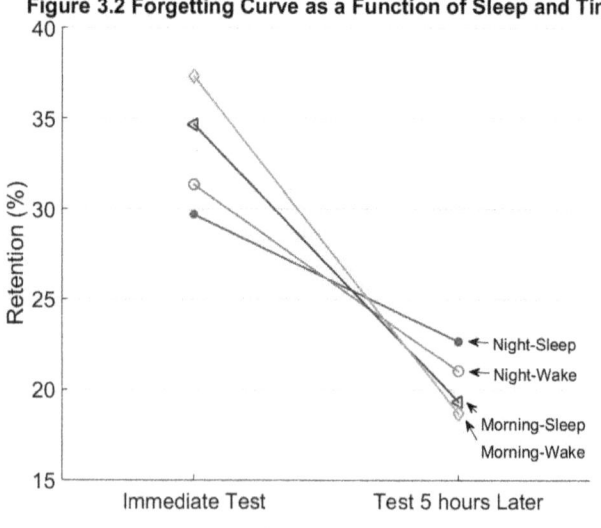

Figure 3.2 Forgetting Curve as a Function of Sleep and Time

Ebbinghaus' Concern: What Is the Use of Sleep?

As can be seen, the two morning groups had better memory immediately after learning. But at the test conducted 5 hours later, the two night groups outperformed the morning groups. Comparing the two sleep groups with the two wake groups shows the same pattern: although the two sleep groups scored lower immediately after learning, they outperformed the two wake groups 5 hours after learning.

We can get two conclusions from this study. First, learning in the morning enhances immediate memory, but learning in the evening brings better memory in the long-run. Second, following learning, sleep enhances memory. Both conclusions prove true by later research.

In another study conducted by British psychologist Simon Folkard in 1977, children aged 12–13 were asked to learn a story about a horse. One group learned it in the morning at 9:00 am, the other group in the afternoon at 3:00 pm. The children answered multiple-choice questions on this story twice, once immediately and once a week later. For the test conducted a week later, for both groups, half were tested at 9:00 am, the other half 3:00 pm. This manipulation controlled the influence of test time.

It was found that at the immediate test, the morning group had better memory than the afternoon group.

However, a week later, irrespective of being tested at 9:00 am or 3:00 pm, the afternoon group consistently outperformed the morning group. The results are shown in Figure 3.3.

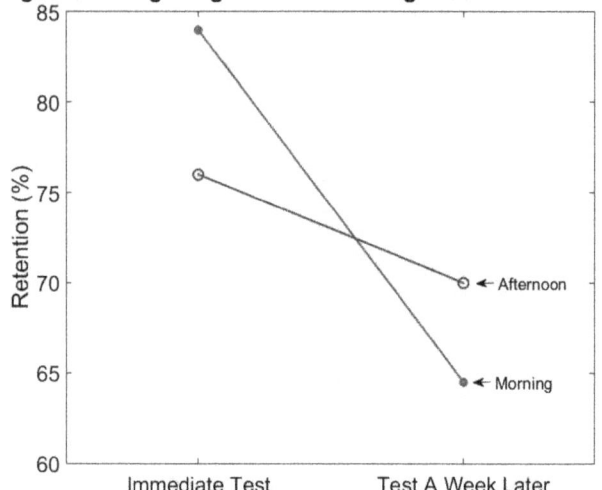

Figure 3.3 Forgetting Curve of Morning vs Afternoon Learning

<u>Learning in the morning brings better immediate memory, but learning in the afternoon or evening brings superior memory in the long run.</u>

James L. McGaugh, a psychologist at the University of California, Irvine, even joked in his 2003 book *Memory and Emotion* that: "My high school and college band rehearsals were all scheduled in the morning, that is why I did not become a professional musician, at least one of many explanations."

This, however, does not suggest that we should abandon learning in the morning altogether. Rather, for learning in the morning, we should use more effective strategies.

Chapter 4
Research Advances on the Process of Memory

Facts may accumulate without theory; but they will prove to be unstable and of little profit in the end. Theories may flourish if their basis lies not in scientific fact but in opinions and interpretations acceptable only to the members of a limited faction; but they will be bad theories...

— Edwin R. Guthrie, *Presidential Address of the American Psychological Association* (1946)

Theories and models are helpful in summarizing and synthesizing a large amount of data. They provide us with generalized, parsimonious knowledge. In this chapter, we look at the progress of theories and models on the process (i.e., the "natural history") of memory.

The flow of information through the memory system

In 1968, Stanford psychologist Richard Atkinson and his student Richard Shiffrin proposed a memory process model that still guides our understanding of memory today.

Research Advances on the Process of Memory

As shown in Figure 4.1, people first attend to and perceive information in the external environment through five senses, such as visual, auditory, and haptic (related to touching) senses. This generates "sensory registers," which are also called sensory memory. Whereas some sensory memory is forgotten and lost, some can be stored in the brain for a short period, called "short-term memory."

Depending on the importance of such information or whether people rehearse it or not, short-term memory is further stored in "long-term memory" or forgotten.

Figure 4.1 The Flow of Information Through the Memory System

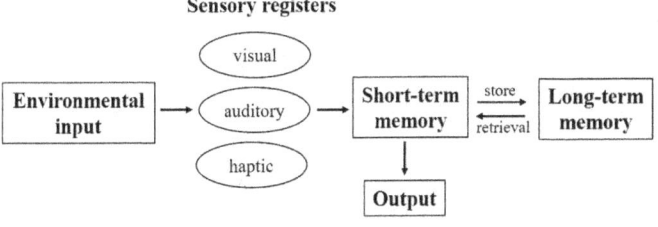

Short-term memory currently active and being manipulated in the brain—it comes from sensory memory or is recalled from long-term memory—is also known as working memory. Working memory is where the brain processes information and produces new outputs, such as an inference, a decision, or an insight.

To more clearly understand memory, it is helpful to differentiate between several kinds of memories.

Declarative and non-declarative memory

According to whether it is available to our conscious mind, memory can be divided into two categories, declarative and non-declarative. Declarative memory is also known as explicit memory and refers to the memory of facts and events ("knowing what"). For instance, your memory of our previous chapters is declarative memory. It can be consciously recalled or declared.

Non-declarative memory, or implicit/procedural memory, refers to the memory of skills particularly motor skills such as riding a bicycle ("knowing how"). Non-declarative memories are primarily acquired through practice and cannot be declared: we are not consciously aware of them.

Perhaps you have noticed, the types of memory we have introduced so far is the declarative memory, as it is the primary form of memory important for work and school. As you continue reading, you will observe that declarative memory is the primary focus of our discussion, while the non-declarative memory is only mentioned occasionally.

Episodic and semantic memory

Within declarative memory, Endel Tulving, a Canadian psychologist at the University of Toronto distinguished between episodic and semantic memory.

The central feature of episodic memory is that both the content of a personal experience ("what") and the context in which it takes place including the time ("when") and place ("where") are stored in memory. You not only remember what we introduce here in this book, but also when and where you read this book. What date and time is it now? And are you at home, work, or in the library?

Semantic memory does not contain the information of time and space. It is a pure, broad understanding of the world. Semantic memory is our generalized knowledge and interpretation of the world.

Often, semantic memory comes from abstracted and decontextualized episodic memory. For instance, we learn about other people through interacting with them. At first, our memory of these interactions is highly contextualized. It is primarily episodic memory. But as the interactions with the same persons increase, we gradually reach more general conclusions about them, and about their personality. These conclusions are semantic memory.

Uncover the memory process: The Hippocampal-Neocortical Interactions Theory

Richard G. Morris, a British neuroscientist at the University of Edinburgh and the inventor of the widely used animal behavior test Morris Water Maze, proposed the Hippocampal-Neocortical Interactions Theory.

This theory is the state-of-the-art integration of our current knowledge on memory. It is based on other scholars' theories such as the Standard Consolidation Theory, Connectionist Model, Multiple Trace Theory, Trace-Transformation Theory, and Schema Assimilation Model and further combined data from many animal and human experiments.

According to this theory, as presented in Figure 4.2 and Table 4.1, the formation of long-term memory requires four stages. Each stage is necessary and has great practical significance in improving memory.

Figure 4.2 Four Stages of the Formation of Long-term Memory

1. Encoding and storage
   ⇩
2. Cellular consolidation
   ⇩
3. Systems consolidation
   ⇩
4. Retrieval and reconsolidation

Stage 1: Encoding and storage

The hippocampus and the neocortex (neural networks outside the hippocampus) encode the learning experience simultaneously. The neocortex encodes more detailed sensory features of information, while the hippocampus encodes the episodic (i.e., "when" and "where") features. Notably, the hippocampus links the memory components encoded by the neocortex together and stores them as specific and vivid long-term memory under the background of time and space (namely episodic memory).

Stage 2: Cellular consolidation

Within minutes to hours of the learning experience, the connections between the neurons of the hippocampus and the neocortex (synaptic connectivity) are enhanced. During this process, memory consolidation is achieved through protein synthesis.

Stage 3: Systems consolidation

During the subsequent days, weeks to months, memory must go through systems consolidation to be stabilized. This is like the theorizing of a large amount of data to form a generalized, parsimonious pattern.

Systems consolidation has two main processes, "abstraction" and "assimilation." Both require the participation of the neocortex.

Through abstraction, the neocortex densifies and abstracts the specific and vivid memories stored in the hippocampus. It stores the repetitive parts of the multiple memories as a general pattern or schema (structural framework, goal plan, see Chapter 10). This process is also called "semantic conversion" as episodic memories are converted to semantic knowledge. The knowledge learned in a certain context can now be generalized and applied independently of the original context (time and space).

Interestingly, when new concepts or information can activate or relate to previous knowledge, patterns, or schemas already stored in the neocortex, systems consolidation can be completed quickly (from minutes to hours). Here, the neocortex, predominantly the prefrontal cortex, guides the hippocampus to encode and store new information. This process is known as "assimilation." An example is when we quickly remember things we are interested in or good at, compared to things we consider boring or unfamiliar.

Stage 4: Retrieval and reconsolidation

Recalling or reactivating, such as testing, pushes the memory back into an unstable state. It, like the new memory, activates cellular processes which need to be further consolidated. Based on the result of the consolidation, memory can be further strengthened, suppressed, or distorted. This stage is also called memory updating because it allows new information to be absorbed and integrated into earlier memory.

Table 4.1 Four Stages of the Formation of Long-term Memory

Stages	Brain region	Psychological process	Physiological process	Duration
1. Encoding and storage	The hippocampus and neocortex	Learning experience, the formation of episodic memory (short-term memory)	Hippocampal synaptic potentiation, the early phase of LTP, protein synthesis-independent	Within 3 hours
2. Cellular consolidation	The hippocampus	Stabilization of memory	The late phase of LTP, protein synthesis-dependent	Minutes to hours
3. Systems consolidation	The hippocampus and neocortex	Transformation of episodic memory into semantic memory; abstraction (extraction of patterns); assimilation (integration into previous knowledge)	The interaction between the hippocampus and neocortex: the connection between different modules within the neocortex; sleep-dependent	Days, weeks, to months
4. Retrieval and reconsolidation	The hippocampus and neocortex	Memory reactivated, either strengthened, weakened (inhibited), or biased (producing wrong memory); memory updating	Reactivation of the cellular mechanisms of memory storage	Hours to days after reactivation

The rest of the book is built under the framework of this theory.

Chapter 5
Revisiting Sleep

In 1994, two neuroscientists Matthew A. Wilson and Bruce L. McNaughton at the University of Arizona discovered the reactivation of memory during sleep. They found that rats' neurons that fired together during the daytime while performing behavioral tasks (such as finding the path to food) become active again during sleep at night. That is, previously learned neural activities reappear during sleep.

This phenomenon soon attracted the attention of other neuroscientists. Further investigation confirmed the same findings when rats explore a new environment. During slow-wave sleep, the hippocampal neural circuit is activated again, and within about 50 milliseconds of this reactivation, areas outside the hippocampus, including the prefrontal cortex, the parietal cortex, the visual cortex, and the striatum show similar neural activity.

Later human neuroimaging studies validated these findings and concluded that sleep supports assimilation and abstraction, two processes of systems consolidation.

Specifically, during sleep, especially during slow-wave sleep, the neural activity that has occurred during the daytime will be repeatedly activated, resulting in the conversion of previously unstable memories to more stable long-term memory. The more stable long-term memory is transferred from the hippocampus to the neocortex, and integrated into previously existing knowledge (assimilation).

Meanwhile, the vivid and specific memories of the previous learning are decontextualized and transformed into more generalized knowledge (abstraction). This process promotes insight (see below).

Subsequent rapid eye movement sleep further stabilizes and consolidates these newly transformed memories.

The critical role of sleep in systems consolidation explains the findings we introduced in Chapter 3.

<u>Learning that occurred closer to sleep will be consolidated earlier and memorized better.</u>

Sleep promotes insight

That sleep promotes insight is excellently illustrated by an experiment conducted by German scientist Ullrich Wagner at the University of Lubeck.

Wagner asked subjects to do a number reduction task, which was transforming a string of digits into a new string with two simple rules. However, a hidden rule, which allowed faster answers, was unknown to the subjects. The subjective realization of the hidden rule required the recognition of patterns, which was supported by the abstraction process of systems consolidation.

Half of the subjects went to sleep for 8 hours after the initial learning; the other half stayed awake. At later retesting, more than twice as many subjects gained insight into the hidden rule after 8 hours of sleep relative to wake.

<u>A whole night of sleep promotes the systems consolidation of information learned on the previous day.</u>

Napping enhances the systems consolidation of memory

Not only normal sleep, a short period of napping also promotes the consolidation of memory after learning.

In a study conducted by German scientist Olaf Lahl at the University of Dusseldorf, subjects were asked to remember 30 adjectives in two minutes at noon. One hour later, they were tested by a free recall test. During this 1-hour period, one group stayed awake and played computer games. A second group napped shortly (around 6 minutes) and then played the same computer game after waking up. A third group napped longer, around 36 minutes. In this experiment, it took about 10 minutes for the subjects to fall asleep. Their results on the test is shown in Figure 5.1.

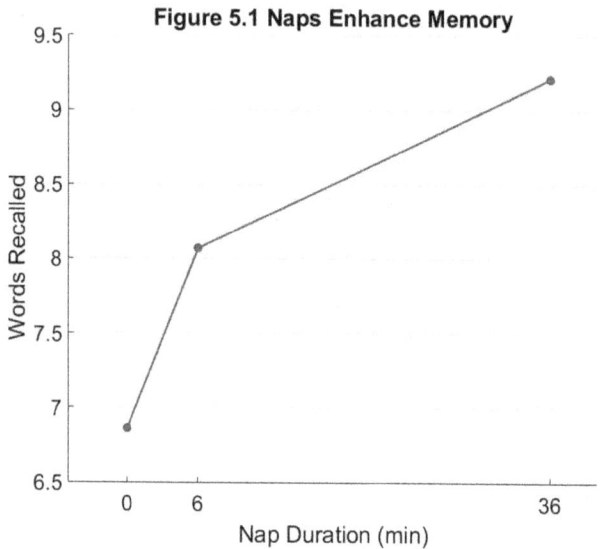

As the duration of napping increased, the number of words recalled also increased.

Napping similarly promotes insight as a full night of sleep. Psychologist Hiuyan Lau at the City College of the City University of New York asked American college students to learn a series of Chinese characters, such as *sister*, *mother*, and *maid* around noon. These characters had the same semantic components called radicals. In the case of *sister*, *mother*, and *maid*, the radical is *female*. Realizing the hidden common semantic component namely the radicals required abstraction of the information and involved the systems consolidation of memory.

Subjects' learning of these characters were tested in two tasks. In the first multiple-choice task, subjects had to guess the meaning of new characters that shared the same radical, such as *princess*. In the radical task, they were explicitly asked the meaning of the radicals.

Following the learning session, half of the students received the test 90 minutes later, during which they either napped (immediate-nap group) or watched an unrelated movie (immediate-wake group). The other half received the test 180 minutes later, during which they either watched an unrelated movie for the whole 180 minutes (delayed-wake group) or watched an unrelated movie for 90 minutes and then napped for 90 minutes (delayed-nap group). Their performance is shown in Figure 5.2.

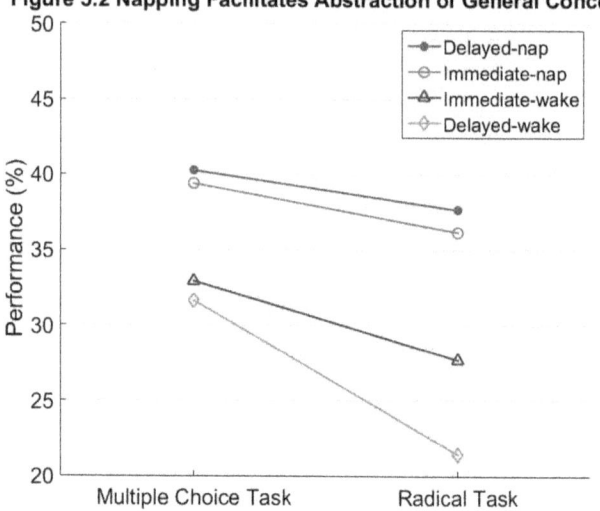

Figure 5.2 Napping Facilitates Abstraction of General Concepts

The two naps groups were more likely to come up with the meaning of the hidden radicals.

<u>Napping after learning promotes systems consolidation.</u>

Sleep deprivation impairs memory of previous learning

As sleep and napping promote systems consolidation, it follows that insufficient sleep compromises memory.

Robert Stickgold at Harvard Medical School asked subjects to practice a visual discrimination task. The improvement of performance on this task was sleep-dependent: subjects did not show improvement on this task on the first day of practice, but did after overnight sleep. This suggested that sleep was necessary for the memory consolidation of this visual discrimination task.

After the first day of practice, Stickgold asked half of the subjects to stay awake for 30 hours and allowed them to freely compensate for sleep during the next two days. This was similar to the situation of people doing night shifts or partying all night on Friday.

Later, when tested on the fourth day, the sleep-deprived subjects only improved by 3.9 milliseconds, while those who slept regularly had improved almost 20 milliseconds, as shown in Figure 5.3.

<u>Sleeping during the first night after learning is necessary for memory consolidation.</u>

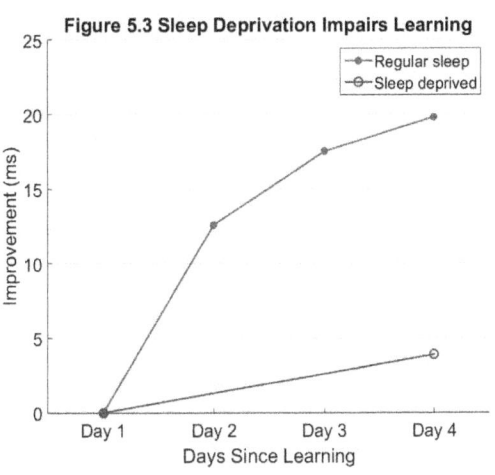

Figure 5.3 Sleep Deprivation Impairs Learning

So it is not a good idea to party all night or stay up for any reason if you value learning and memory. But when you do, you'd better spend extra time reviewing what you have learned.

Sleep deprivation impairs subsequent learning

Sleep deprivation changes the normal functioning of the brain including the hippocampus and the neocortex. Therefore, it also impairs the subsequent encoding and storage of new information.

In one study conducted by British scientists in the 1980s, twelve physicians were tested after three conditions: a night off duty; a night on call; a night spent admitting emergency cases. Notably, during a night shift particularly a night spent admitting emergency cases, physicians have only limited and fragmented sleep.

In the test, the physicians first read a text and then were asked to recall the contents. Their scores are shown in Figure 5.4. After a night spent admitting emergency cases, the physicians had the poorest capacity to remember new information (i.e., short-term memory).

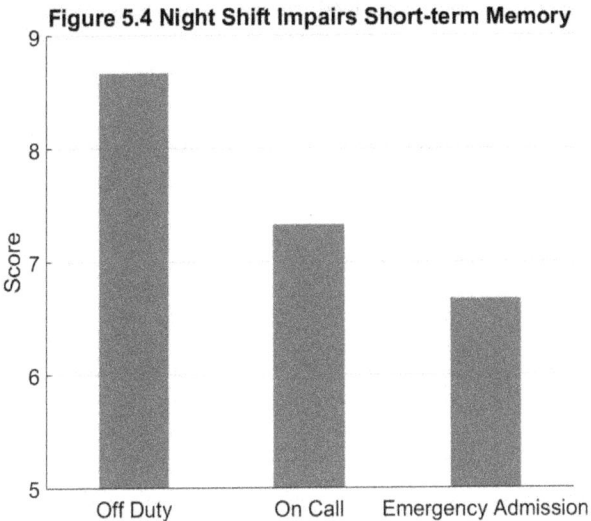

Figure 5.4 Night Shift Impairs Short-term Memory

In another study conducted by scientists at the University of California, San Diego, after learning a series of word lists, people deprived of sleep for 35 hours could only recall about 60% of the words recalled by people who slept regularly (Figure 5.5).

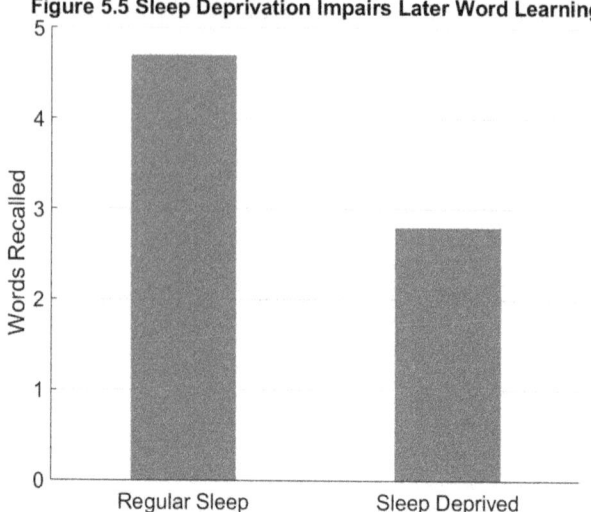
Figure 5.5 Sleep Deprivation Impairs Later Word Learning

<u>Sleep deprivation not only impairs the consolidation of previous memory, it also compromises the later encoding and storage of new information.</u>

PART 2
The Encoding and Storage of Memory

CHAPTER 6
Things Are Better Remembered When We Pay Attention

Atkinson and Shiffrin's classic model of the process of memory (sensory register → short-term memory → long-term memory) holds that information must be stored in short-term memory for a period of time before it enters long-term memory. In line with this, information that stays in short-term memory longer will be remembered better, because it uses more encoding resources. Rehearsal prolongs the storage of information in short-term memory and thus enhances long-term memory.

Meanwhile, information has to first enter our attention before it is processed in the short-term memory (or more specifically, working memory). That is, attention gates short-term memory. As such, compared to incidental memory, things are better remembered when we pay attention. This explains why people with focus issues often have poor memory.

Intentional memory lasts longer than incidental memory

In one study, subjects were explicitly asked to remember eight surnames. Besides, they were presented three additional groups of eight surnames, but without being explicitly told that they had to remember them.

For the first group, they had to indicate the first letter (physical/visual feature). For the second group, they were asked to come up with a word with similar pronunciation (phonological). For the third group, they had to use the words to make a sentence (semantic). For the three additional groups of surnames, their memory was an incidental memory.

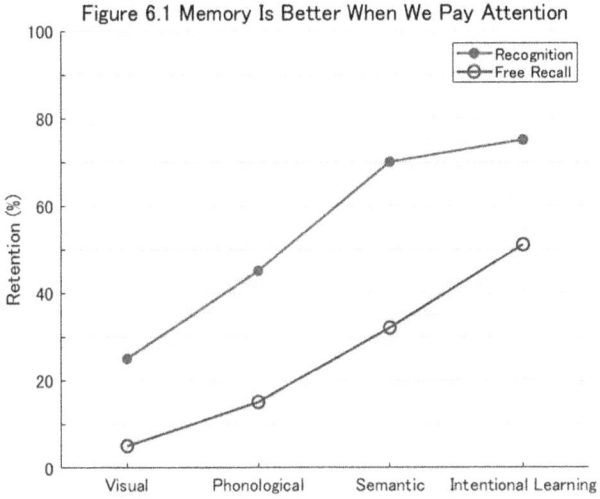

Figure 6.1 Memory Is Better When We Pay Attention

As shown in Figure 6.1, in a later test, intentional learning resulted in the best memory.

<u>Things are better remembered when we intentionally try to memorize them.</u>

Among the incidental memories, the memory effect of semantic processing is better than phonological judgement, which is better than judgement based on physical forms. This phenomenon is known as the Levels of Processing Theory.

The Levels of Processing Theory

In 1972, the same year when Endel Tulving differentiated the concept of semantic from episodic memory, his colleagues Fergus Craik and Robert Lockhart at the University of Toronto put forward the Levels of Processing Theory. They argued that information processed at a deeper level brings better long-term memory.

During the encoding process, the depth of information processing determines how much information is stored in long-term memory. The depth of information processing refers to the degree of encoding in terms of the involvement of sensory registers and semantic meaning.

When we learn a new word, we first notice its visual or auditory features, such as its strokes, lines, pronunciation, and loudness. Next, we will understand its meaning and use it in reasoning and application. The three levels from visual to auditory to meaning deepen layer by layer.

Purely visual features (text) are superficial; auditory features will bring deeper processing. However, when we understand the semantic meaning of information (e.g., words), it is a further deeper level of information processing.

<u>Auditory features are at a deeper level than visual features because auditory memory (which is also called "echoic memory") is more durable and lasts longer than visual memory. That is, auditory features stay longer in short-term memory and use more encoding resources than visual features.</u>

<u>Semantic features are further deeper because when we pay attention to the meaning of new information, it is likely to activate associated knowledge and connect with our previous similar experiences related to the meaning.</u>

When we use prior knowledge we have learned, the level of information processing becomes deeper. Deeper processing brings lasting, solid memory traces. Therefore, highly familiar information will more easily lead to deep processing.

The Levels of Processing Theory was built upon research of word lists. But it has practical implications beyond learning of new language. The notion that information that activates more, deeper semantic network is remembered better explains the superior memory effect of schema-guided learning (Part 3). Semantic information that activates more previous knowledge or schema is processed at a deeper level.

The Distinctiveness Effect

Another example illustrating that attention enhances memory is the Distinctiveness Effect, which is also known as the Isolation or von Restorff Effect.

As first reported by German psychiatrist Hedwig von Restorff, when presented a list of categorically similar items with one isolated, distinctive item on the list, people remember the distinctive item better compared to the rest items.

Isolated or special entries and information are treated as if they are a single category. Compared with the background entry category (less distinctive counterparts), this single category attracts more attention and more encoding resources. Therefore, it is better remembered.

<u>Distinctive information attracts more attention and is remembered better.</u>

The Distinctiveness Effect explains many observations. When we come across a stranger, we remember his face better if he has a unique name. Similarly, we recall a stranger's name easier if he has a distinctive face. Look at any well prepared pamphlets or advertisements. The authors all try to make the most important information stand out and catch our attention.

Highlighting and underlining

Highlighted, underlined, or capitalized sentences are distinctive among regular texts, and will pop out and draw more attention. Several studies have shown that:

<u>People are more likely to remember marked sentences in a text.</u>

Educational scientist James H. Crouse and Peter Idstein asked college students to read an article "Education and Philosophical Thoughts." Half of the students read a regular version, while the other half read a version with the important contents underlined. After reading, everyone studied the text at their own pace for 25 minutes. In a later test, irrespective of their original learning abilities, those who read the underlined version scored higher than those who read the regular version.

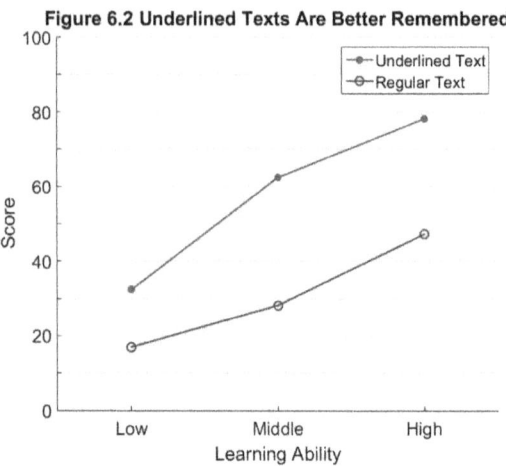

Figure 6.2 Underlined Texts Are Better Remembered

Interestingly, compared to merely reading highlighted texts, highlighting the text oneself results in even better learning.

In another study, educational scientist John P. Rickards and Gerald J. August asked college students to read an article about brain evolution. Some students read a marked version of the text with its important contents underscored. The others read the regular version but were asked to underline the single most important sentence in each paragraph.

It was found that compared to those who read the marked version of the article, those underlining the article themselves recalled more items (including those not underlined, see Figure 6.3).

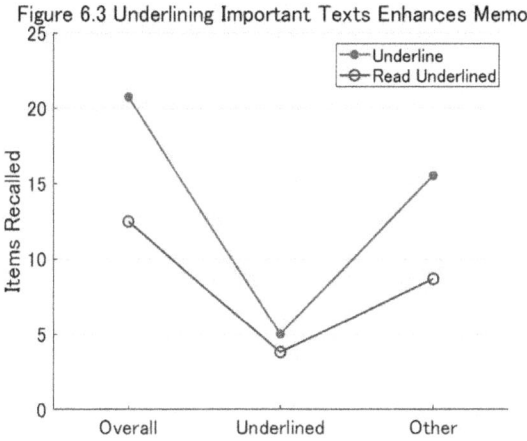

Figure 6.3 Underlining Important Texts Enhances Memory

Surveys show that irrespective of reading ability, students often use highlighting as a learning strategy. However, whereas students with a high reading ability only mark a few, important pieces of information, those with a poor reading ability often mark a lot of information.

Here, to underline the most important information, one must first understand the whole text and judge what is most important. This involves deep, semantic processing of the contents.

<u>Highlighting a few most important pieces of information in a text promotes a deep level of processing and enhances memory.</u>

CHAPTER 7
Multiple Modes of Encoding

Many studies have reported the phenomenon that when learning new words, reading aloud enhances memory more than reading silently. This is the Production Effect.

For instance, in a study conducted by Noah D. Forrin at the University of Waterloo, subjects were asked to learn new words with different methods. For some of the words, subjects read them out loud in a normal speaking voice. For some, subjects read them at a whisper or only mouthed the words. For others, subjects wrote them down, but erased them immediately. Still, for others, subjects merely read in their mind.

In a later recognition test, it was found that the best-remembered words were those read aloud, as shown in Figure 7.1.

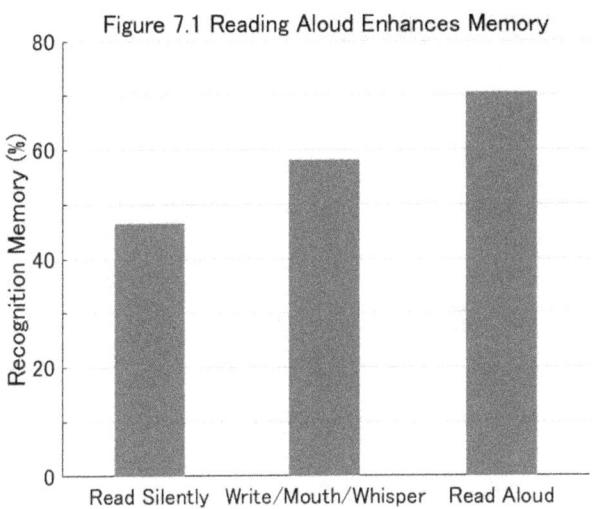

When learning new words, writing, mouthing, and whispering produce more robust memory compared to reading silently because they involve additional modes or channels of encoding: manual movement, articulation, and audition. Reading aloud enhances memory even more as it produces a sound that activates auditory processing to a greater extent.

In the same token, singing provides another mode of encoding: rhythm and melody. Therefore, singing enhances the memory of lyrics.

Psychologist Wanda T. Wallace asked subjects to listen to three previously unfamiliar folk ballads. The first ballad was the original song, the second was read aloud with the same melody, and the third was just read aloud. Subjects were tested on their memory of the lyrics after listening for 1, 2, and 5 times as well as 20 minutes following the 5th time (a delayed test). All the tests were carried out in the form of free recall tests.

As shown in Figure 7.2, those who listened to the original song consistently performed the best, while those listening to the read-aloud version with the melody outperformed those listening to the lyrics alone.

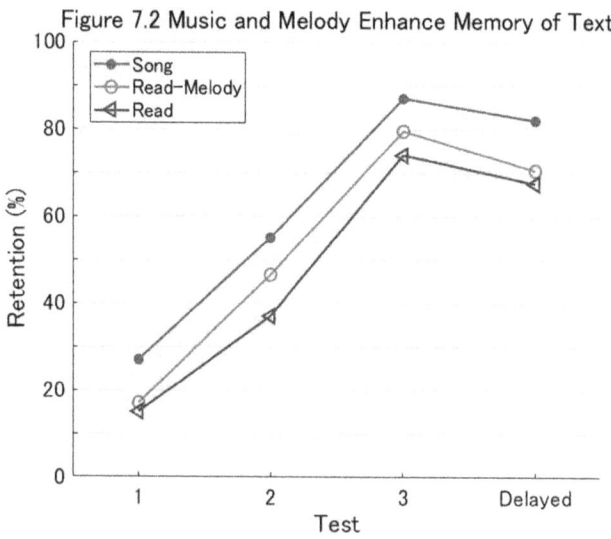

Figure 7.2 Music and Melody Enhance Memory of Text

Music and melody also help people learn foreign languages. Karen M. Ludke at the University of Edinburgh let native English speakers learn English-Hungarian phrase pairs. Subjects first heard the English words and then the

Hungarian phrases twice. After that, they had to repeat the Hungarian words aloud.

For the first group of subjects, the Hungarian phrases were read by a native Hungarian speaker (Speaking). For the second group, the phrases were spoken by the same person but embedded in the rhythm of Hungarian folk songs without the melody line (Rhythmic Speaking). For the third group, the words were sung by the person with the melodic line (Singing).

When later asked to recall the Hungarian words, those in the singing group had the best performance.

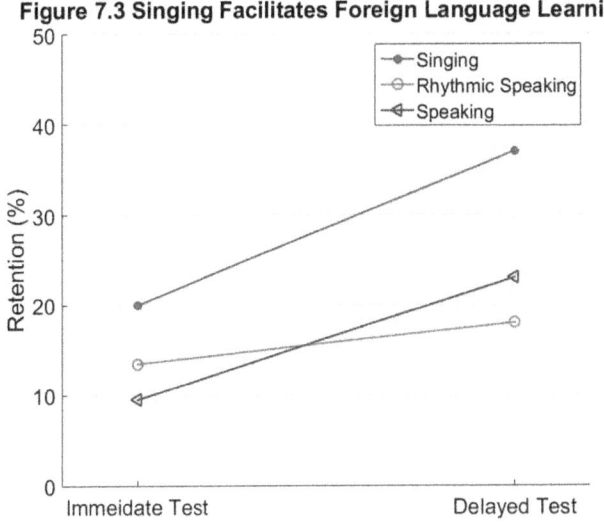

Figure 7.3 Singing Facilitates Foreign Language Learning

Strategic Memory

Listening to and singing songs promote memory of the lyrics. This can be used to learn a foreign language.

Chapter 8
The Modality Effect and Multimedia Learning

Things are better remembered when we pay attention. However, our attention span is limited. We can only attend to a limited amount of information at a time. We have two primary modes of encoding: visual and auditory. Each mode has a limited capacity of processing information.

Therefore, optimizing incoming information by balancing its presentation in different modes (e.g., combining visual imagery with auditory information) reduces the memory load and frees working memory. It leaves more space for the actual learning process (encoding). In line with this, in the 1960s, L.R. Brooks discovered that:

<u>If people are given a complex message to visualize, the memory of the message is better if it is presented auditorily as opposed to visually.</u>

Including visual material interferes with the visualization process, as both require visual processing and our capacity of a single mode of processing is limited. This phenomenon is known as the Modality Effect.

The Modality Effect is well illustrated by an experiment conducted by Joel R. Levin and Patricia Divine-Hawkins at the University of Wisconsin. They asked children to read or listen to sentences describing monkeys and cars. Half of them had to visualize the sentences. The children then answered 10 questions regarding the contents of the sentences. As shown in Figure 8.1, those who listened to the sentences and visualized the contents had the best memory.

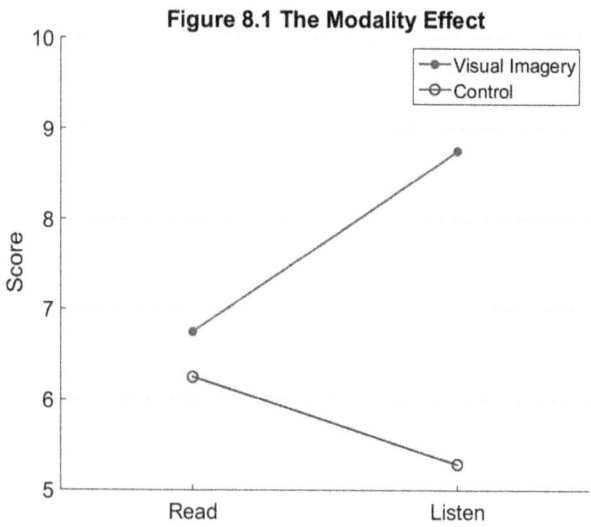

The now popular multimedia learning is designed based on the Modality Effect. It proves to be an effective strategy to enhance memory.

The Modality Effect and Multimedia Learning

Australian educational scientist John Sweller at the University of New South Wales studied the process of learning the congruent law of triangles in geometry by junior high school students. The law states that if the three sides of the two triangles are equal, then the two triangles are congruent triangles and can coincide.

During the study of explanatory examples, the first group of students could simultaneously hear the voice recorder playing the text explanation while seeing the chart and the corresponding text explanation (Audio-Visual Synchronization). The second group could see the chart and the corresponding text explanation (Visual-Visual). The third group only saw the chart and simultaneously heard the voice recorder playing the text explanation (Visual-Auditory).

After learning two examples, students were asked to solve two other similar questions and two transfer questions in different contexts. As shown in Figure 8.2, the Visual-Auditory group took the least time solving the problems.

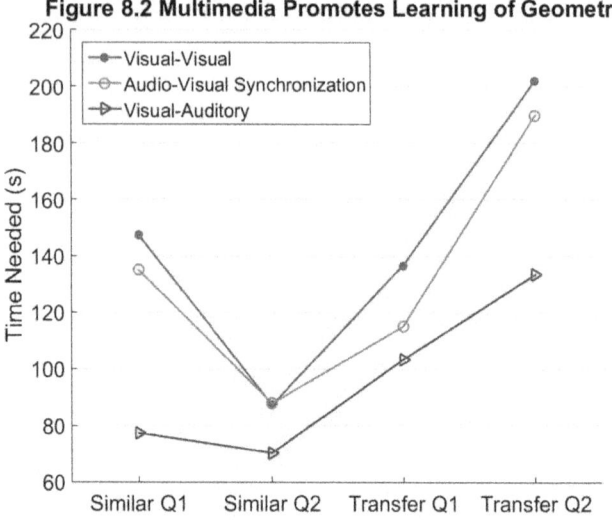

Figure 8.2 Multimedia Promotes Learning of Geometry

In another study, Richard E. Mayer and Roxana Moreno at the University of California, Santa Barbara, showed that multimedia promotes students' learning of geographical knowledge. In this study, college students watched the animation of the formation of lightning, including the movement of air currents from the ocean to the land, the condensation of water vapor to form clouds, the elevation of the clouds until they exceed freezing levels, the formation of crystals in the clouds, and so on.

While watching the animation, half of the students heard a male voice simultaneously describing important information in the animation. The other half simultaneously saw the same text message on the screen.

The students later received three tests: one recall test to explain the formation of the lightning; one matching test to recognize certain concepts and activities during the formation of the lightning from corresponding diagrams; one knowledge transfer test answering questions such as what caused the lightning and so on.

Across all three tests, those who watched the animation while hearing the explanation performed better. The result is shown in Figure 8.3.

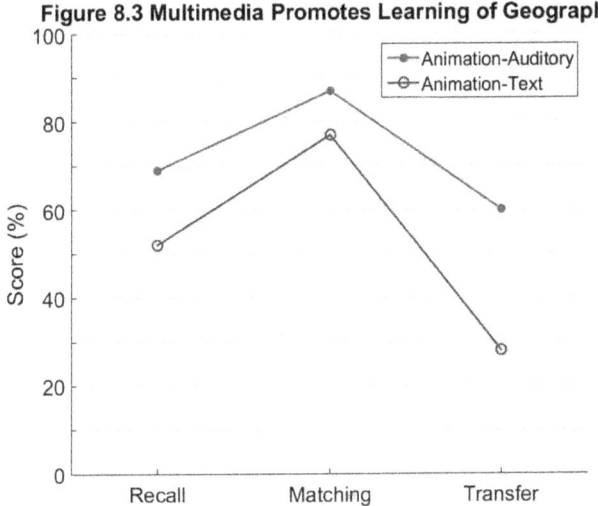

Carefully designed multimedia learning, in which people form a mental representation from illustrative pictures or animations combined with auditory explanatory information, enhances memory.

PART 3
Schema and Systems Consolidation

CHAPTER 9
How Prior Knowledge Changes Learning

When new information or concepts can activate previous knowledge already stored in the neocortex, the neocortex guides the hippocampus in encoding new incoming information. Here, systems consolidation finishes quickly, leading to more stable memory.

A study conducted by James F. Voss at the University of Pittsburgh provided robust evidence. Voss tested the reading comprehension ability of students in a junior high school and selected those with scores at the highest 70% and the lowest 30%. He then sorted these students according to their knowledge level of baseball.

Therefore, 4 groups were studied in this research: good readers with high level of baseball knowledge; good readers with low level of baseball knowledge; poor readers with high level of baseball knowledge; and poor readers with low level of baseball knowledge. Voss asked these 4 groups of students to read an essay describing a baseball game and then let them use a model to reproduce the game and describe the game with their own language.

The results showed that both reading ability and baseball knowledge affected the final performance.

Students with higher reading ability and more baseball knowledge were better able to reproduce the game using a model and describe it with their own language. Interestingly, the impact of baseball knowledge was higher than reading ability.

For instance, as can be seen from Figure 9.1, for the same level of baseball knowledge, the improvement in the modeling score (i.e., the ability to reproduce the game using a model) because of reading ability was 9.75 (knowledge was high) and 12.25 (knowledge was low). For the same level of reading ability, the improvement in the modeling score because of baseball knowledge was 31.5 (high reading ability) and 34 (low reading ability).

The conclusion is more obvious if we notice those with high levels of baseball knowledge but poor at reading outperformed those good at reading but with low levels of baseball knowledge.

<u>High levels of knowledge can compensate for poor reading ability.</u>

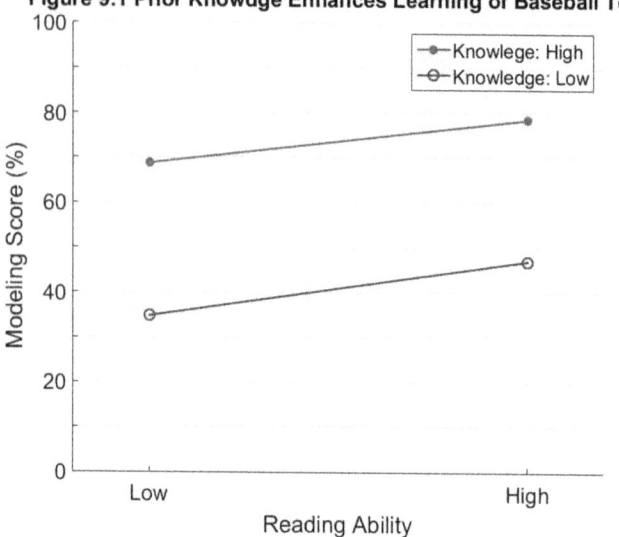

Figure 9.1 Prior Knowdge Enhances Learning of Baseball Text

More detailed analysis showed those with high levels of baseball knowledge were better able to recall the setting and actions of the game.

Another example was provided by Danielle S. McNamara and Walter Kintsch. They presented two versions of a text on the Vietnam War to American subjects. These two versions differed in their coherence so one version employed the names of places and armies familiar to the American subjects (high-coherence).

For instance, two sentences in the high-coherence version were:

"By the beginning of 1965, American officials in both South Vietnam and the U.S. had begun to focus on North Vietnam as the source of the continuing war in South Vietnam. The South Vietnamese army was losing the ground war against North Vietnam and this caused frustrations among the American officials."

These sentences in the low-coherence version were:

"By the fall of 1964, Americans in both Saigon and Washington had begun to focus on Hanoi as the source of the continuing problem in the south. As frustrations mounted over the inability of the ARVN to defeat the enemy in the field, pressure to strike directly at North Vietnam began to build."

For people with low levels of knowledge on Vietnam, the low-coherence version makes little sense. They can hardly figure out what is meant by Saigon, Hanoi, and ARVN. They cannot get coherent information from this version of the text. In line with this, it was found that one week after reading the text, those with high levels of knowledge on Vietnam recalled more information and performed better on open-ended comprehension questions. The result of the recall test is shown in Figure 9.2.

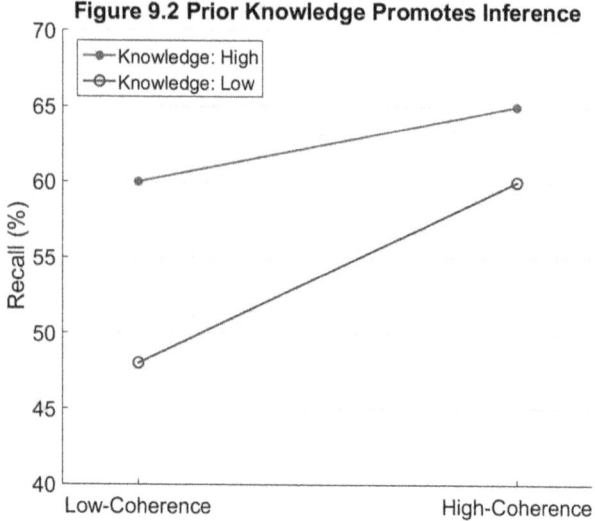

Figure 9.2 Prior Knowledge Promotes Inference

<u>Prior knowledge helps people identify meaning and extract patterns from novel information. It activates existing schemas and dramatically accelerates the systems consolidation of memory.</u>

Other research suggests that when reading novel information within one's expertise, people are more likely to use deep processing strategies, such as overviewing before settling in to read, summarizing and connecting to their prior knowledge (see Chapter 11 and 12). They are more likely to combine their prior knowledge with cues from the material to generate predictions and navigate within the material (goal-directed reading).

The benefits of extensive reading

If we have accumulated an extensive amount of knowledge, then when we come across relevant material later, we can better learn and memorize the new material.

British educational scientist K.J. Topping at the University of Dundee analyzed data of over 45,000 students in grade 1–12 in 139 schools. Topping first tested the reading comprehension ability of these students and then asked them to freely read e-books in the virtual library the researchers established. After reading each book, an immediate test evaluated their reading quality (reading comprehension). A year later, all the students were tested over their reading ability again.

Over the 1-year period, these students read over 3 million books. This was about 1.3 books per student per week. Irrespective of the students' initial reading comprehension ability, their quantity (number of books) and quality of reading were both positively correlated with the changes of reading ability across the 1-year period. Although the impact of reading quality was higher than reading quantity.

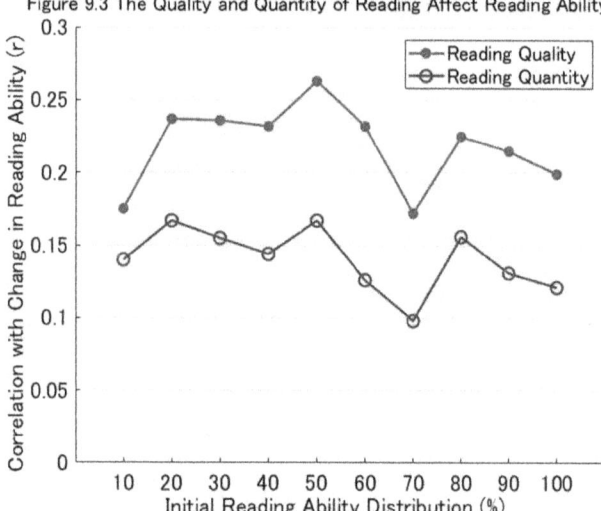

Figure 9.3 The Quality and Quantity of Reading Affect Reading Ability

<u>The more books you read and the better you understand each book you read, the higher your reading ability will be.</u>

Chapter 10
Schemas

Prior knowledge promotes learning because new information can activate schemas that enhance systems consolidation.

The word schema was coined by Immanuel Kant and popularized in psychology and education by British psychologist Frederick C. Bartlett.

Briefly speaking, a schema is a generalized knowledge structure or pattern. It is like a personal "theory" or mental model of the surrounding world (whether or not it is true). Paradigms, theories, principles, laws, worldviews, frames, scripts, archetypes, and stereotypes are all examples of schemas.

We use schemas to interpret, organize, and predict new information and make inferences. As the result of the accumulation of new knowledge, our schemas may change themselves. When novel information is irrelevant to previous knowledge, it may form new schemas.

Even when people have similar levels of knowledge, those have their schemas activated will be better at learning new information.

For instance, please read this description:

"The procedure is actually quite simple. First you arrange things into different groups depending on their makeup. Of course, one pile may be sufficient depending on how much there is to do. If you have to go somewhere else due to lack of facilities that is the next step, otherwise you are pretty well set. It is important not to overdo any particular endeavor. That is, it is better to do too few things at once than too many. In the short run this may not seem important, but complications from doing too many can easily arise. A mistake can be expensive as well. The manipulation of the appropriate mechanisms should be self-explanatory, and we need not dwell on it here. At first the whole procedure will seem complicated. Soon, however, it will become just another facet of life. It is difficult to foresee any end to the necessity for this task in the immediate future, but then one never can tell."

Using a scale of 1 (very difficult) to 7 (very easy), how do you evaluate the ease of understanding this text?

After rating, please recall the entire text as accurately as you can and write down the most important part.

Challenging, isn't it?

Schemas

John D. Bransford and Marcia K. Johnson at the State University of New York asked a group of people to read the above text, rate the ease of reading, and recall it. The average ease-to-understand rating was 2.29, indicating that the text was not so easy to understand. The average score of recalling the text was 16%, relatively poor.

Bransford and Johnson then asked a second group of people to read the text, before which Bransford and Johnson told them that the passage was about washing clothes.

Washing clothes, did you think of it? Now go back and read the text again. It is more comprehensible, isn't it?

The second group found the text much easier to read, with an average rating of 4.50. Meanwhile, they wrote down twice as much contents compared to the first group: their average score of recall was 32%.

This is the power of context. Knowing the text is about washing clothes will activate our schema of using washing machines in everyday life. Such a schema helps to link new information to our prior experience.

Semantic context promotes systems consolidation

Similarly, when the background of new information is provided, our memory of the new information will be enhanced.

Gary L. Bradshaw and John R. Anderson, two psychologists at Carnegie-Mellon University, asked subjects to read the autobiographical information of 28 historical figures including Newton. A week later, people were asked to judge whether certain items were the original factual information they had read.

The autobiographical information was of four kinds:

First, purely factual information, for instance, *Newton became emotionally unstable and insecure as a child.*

Second, besides the factual information, two additional items of irrelevant information were provided. For instance, *Newton was appointed Chief Inspector of the London Mint*; *Newton entered Trinity College of Cambridge.*

Third, besides the factual information, two additional items of information that explained its reason were provided. For instance, *at Newton's birth, his father died*; *Newton's mother married again and left Newton to his grandfather.*

Fourth, besides the factual information, two additional items of information that showed its outcome were provided. For instance, *Newton became extremely paranoid when challenged by a colleague*; *Newton collapsed emotionally when his mother died.*

The result of their memory of the four kinds of information is shown in Figure 10.1.

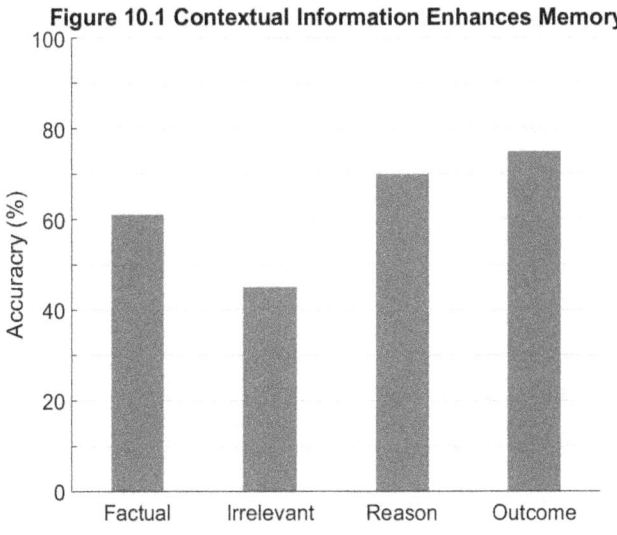

Figure 10.1 Contextual Information Enhances Memory

Subjects' memory of the factual information differed according to what additional information was provided. Irrelevant information interfered with the factual information and reduced memory. Information on the reason and outcome of the factual information enhanced memory, as they provided a context and promoted systems consolidation.

<u>Bringing information into context enhances memory.</u>

Analogical learning and chunking

Analogical learning and chunking are two examples of the practical use of schemas in learning.

<u>Analogies help us understand how a new system works by relating it to a familiar one.</u>

Psychologists found that some students use the analogy of a water-flow system to understand the electrical circuit. The wires are like pipes, battery pump, electrons water, and resistor constriction in a pipe.

Chunking is most well-known in the study of chess players. In a famous study, a grand master, a Class A player (whose chance of beating a grand master is estimated to be around 1 in 1,000), and a beginner were asked to spend 5 seconds looking at a board of game before reproducing it. In five different chess sets which had about 24–26 pieces each, the grand master could on average reconstruct 16 pieces correctly; the Class A player 8 pieces; the beginner 4 pieces.

Schemas

It turns out that the grand masters play chess using a chunking strategy. They look at the board in a chunk fashion by associating pieces of confrontation, proximity, or the like with each other. They process and store the information of the pieces in chunks. When asked to reproduce a board, they also put the pieces on the board in this chunk way.

<u>This chunking strategy allows people to remember new information efficiently.</u>

Chunking is mostly studied in decision-making in natural scenes. So we will not go into details about it. If you are interested, please refer to another book of mine: *The Tale of Two Minds: The Art and Science of Decision-making in Everyday Life* (2018).

Chapter 11
Meaningful Learning

Of two men with the same outward experiences and the same amount of mere native tenacity, the one who thinks over his experiences most and weaves them into systematic relations with each other will be the one with the best memory.

— William James, *Principles of Psychology* (1890)

In the 1950–1960s, psychologist David P. Ausubel put forward the Assimilation Theory. He argued that our cognitive structure is hierarchical. The upper layers locate general, abstract, and inclusive concepts, while the lower layers locate special, concrete concepts. When new, meaningful material can be incorporated into the existing concepts in our hierarchical cognitive structure, it is meaningful learning. Ausubel called this process "assimilation." This is essentially a process of systems consolidation.

In contrast to rote learning, when meaningful learning occurs, the connections between related concepts become clearer, more specific, and better integrated. The differences between concepts also become more apparent and some contradictory and ambiguous meaning will disappear. Therefore, meaningful learning is more likely to bring creative results.

Advance organizers

Based on the Assimilation Theory, Ausubel proposed that to promote meaningful learning or the assimilation process, teachers should first provide learners with a preview or advance organizer before explaining new knowledge.

<u>The advance organizer incorporates new knowledge into a systematic framework, which emphasizes the relationship between new concepts and the learners' prior knowledge, particularly those at the upper layers of the cognitive structure. The advance organizer will activate, enhance, or even reorganize the existing knowledge framework—schemas—to promote the understanding of new knowledge. This brings meaningful learning.</u>

The advance organizer provides not simply a context, but a structured context that helps organize and incorporate new information.

In one study, Ausubel asked undergraduates of the psychology department to read a scientific essay on the metallurgical properties of plain carbon steels. The essay was about 2,500 words and emphasized the relationship between the structure of metal grain with temperature, carbon content and cooling rate. This was a novel, unfamiliar topic to students majored in psychology. So the study could reflect the real situation in which people learn new knowledge.

Notably, before reading this scientific essay, half of the students read another short essay on the similarities and differences between metals and alloys, including their respective strengths and weaknesses, and the reasons for the manufacture and use of alloys. The other half of the students read a short essay on the history of iron and steel processing methods.

Whereas the latter essay provided general background information to stimulate the students' interest, the former was at the upper layer of the cognitive structure. The former was more general, abstract, and inclusive in terms of its information on metal grain and carbon steels. Therefore, those who read the former essay should be better able to organize the subsequent 2,500-word scientific essay on the metallurgical properties of plain carbon steels.

It was found that at the test conducted three days later, those who read the former essay on the similarities and differences between metals and alloys recalled more information from the subsequent scientific essay. The former essay served as an advance organizer that enhanced later learning.

Concept mapping

Since the 1970s, based on the Assimilation Theory, Joseph D. Novak at Cornell University further developed the theory of concept mapping.

<u>Concept mapping involves the conversion of knowledge and information into a map. The map emphasizes the hierarchical relationship between concepts and between concepts and prior knowledge.</u>

A concept map is usually depicted in a diagram or flowchart. Concepts and knowledge are shown as points or concept nodes, which are connected with each other by lines. Labels are then added to the lines to define the relationship between concepts.

The concept map has been called "knowledge map" by other researchers and "mind map" by English folk psychologist Tony Buzan.

In one study, Novak instructed half of grade 1 elementary students to draw a concept map of the science curriculum. The instruction consisted of 28 20-minute sessions and was delivered at the extracurricular time such as during rest or lunch breaks. Novak then tested the comprehension of science concepts when the students were at grade 2, 7, 10, and 12 and also asked them to construct new concept maps.

It was found that those who received concept map instruction at grade 1 could understand the science concepts more accurately throughout the follow-up period. Meanwhile, analyzing the concept maps the students drew suggested that, those who received instruction at grade 1 included more validated concepts, as shown in Figure 11.1.

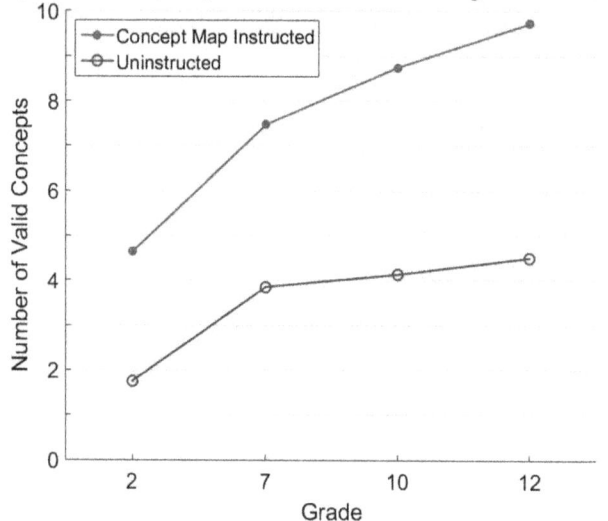

Figure 11.1 Concept Map Instruction Enhances Learning of Science Concepts

The not-for-profit organization The Institute for Human & Machine Cognition has developed concept map tools for use on Windows, OSX, Linux, and iPad, which are easy to use. You can access https://cmap.ihmc.us/cmaptools/ to learn more about this.

German psychologist Tatjana S. Hilbert at the University of Freiburg studied the concept maps drawn by college students and found that the number of concept nodes increases as the knowledge of students increases. Meanwhile, both the number of concept nodes and correctly labeled links are associated with the students' ability to integrate knowledge.

Canadian educational scientist John C. Nesbit and Olusola O. Adesope performed a meta-analysis of 67 studies and concluded that:

<u>Studying concept maps prepared by teachers results in better learning outcomes than traditional learning methods such as those using texts, lists, and outlines or attending lectures and group discussions.</u>

This is true for elementary and high school students, and for many subjects including science, physics, biology, statistics, law, and so on.

<u>Compared to simply studying the concept maps prepared by teachers, constructing concept maps by students themselves has more beneficial learning outcomes. The latter involves deeper processing and more activation of prior knowledge.</u>

CHAPTER 12
Elaborative Encoding That Promotes Systems Consolidation

Besides advance organizers and concept maps, educational scientists have studied many other learning strategies. These strategies require elaborate encoding, which uses prior knowledge and schemas to incorporate new information or extracts patterns from new information. In other words, they promote systems consolidation.

Note-taking

<u>To take notes during learning, we usually need to structure the contents, sort out the most important information, and write them down. This process involves a deep level of semantic processing and also multiple modes of encoding (writing besides reading and/or listening).</u>

Psychologist Gilles O. Einstein at Furman University asked psychology students to watch a 10-minute teaching video about the historical development of individual differences. Half of those students were asked to take notes while watching the video. Later in the free recall test, it was found that compared to those who did not take notes, those who took notes recalled more important contents.

Figure 12.1 Note-taking Enhances Memory of Important Contents

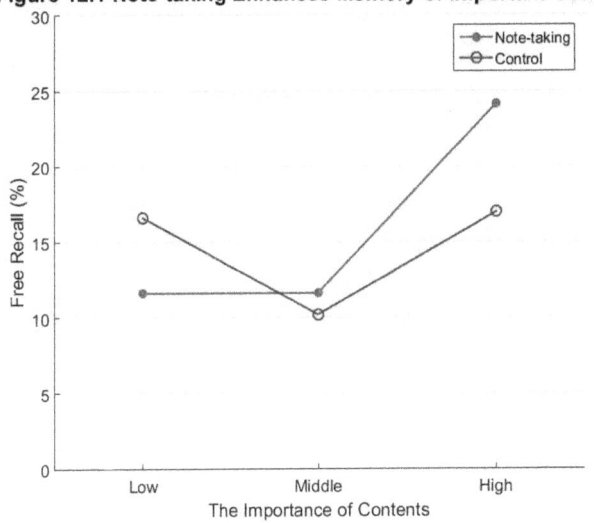

Gilles O. Einstein further analyzed the students' notes and found that:

Compared to those with poor academic achievement, those with high academic achievement recorded more important contents in their notes.

Drawing and making illustrations

One way of taking notes is drawing and making diagrams, illustrations, and hierarchical representations. These are known as visualization strategies.

Concept mapping is in fact one example of these strategies.

Strategic Memory

Psychologist Peggy Van Meter at Pennsylvania State University asked 5th and 6th-grade elementary school students to read a science text on the central nervous system. The text was about two pages long and covered topics of the components of the central nervous system, neurons, and how impulses are transmitted.

After reading the text, the first group of students read two illustrations about the text prepared by researchers.

The second group was asked to draw two illustrations themselves.

The third group was asked to draw two illustrations themselves, after which they read the two illustrations prepared by the researchers and were asked to compare how their drawings differed from those by the researchers.

The fourth group also drew two illustrations themselves and read two illustrations by the researchers, but after which they were asked to systematically compare their own and the researchers' illustrations and answer several questions about the difference.

In a later free recall test, it was found that compared to those who simply read the illustrations, those who draw the illustrations themselves had better memory. Among those who drew the illustrations, those who also systematically compared their own drawing with the researchers' drawing recalled the greatest number of items.

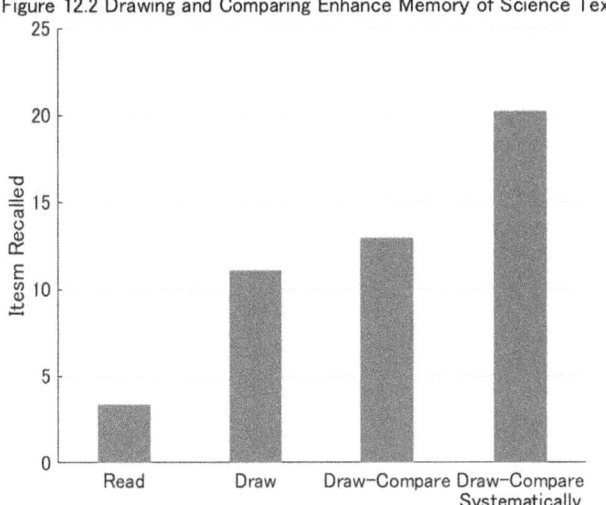

Figure 12.2 Drawing and Comparing Enhance Memory of Science Texts

Summarization

Writing a summary of the learning material is another strategy to improve memory.

<u>Summarization typically involves three processes. First, extracting important information and filtering out the unimportant.</u>

<u>Second, concentrating, structuring, and organizing the important information. This requires people to make connections and integrations to form a high level of thought.</u>

<u>Third, describing the high level of thoughts in a unified, harmonious, parsimonious way, which can accurately represent the original material.</u>

<u>These processes require extra encoding effort and contribute to enhanced memory.</u>

Educational scientist Merlin C. Wittrock at UCLA conducted extensive studies of the learning effect of summarization. He asked elementary school students to read a story in a textbook, high school students to read a science text, and college students to read a book chapter related to their major. Half of the students had to summarize the main ideas after reading. It was found that the students who summarized the main ideas consistently scored higher on later tests of memory and comprehension.

For instance, in one study, Wittrock asked high school students to read a text, after which they had to write a summary of it. Wittrock then asked a second group of students to read the same text and the summary written by the first group. It turned out the first group who wrote the summary outperformed the second group on later tests of facts and inferences based on the text.

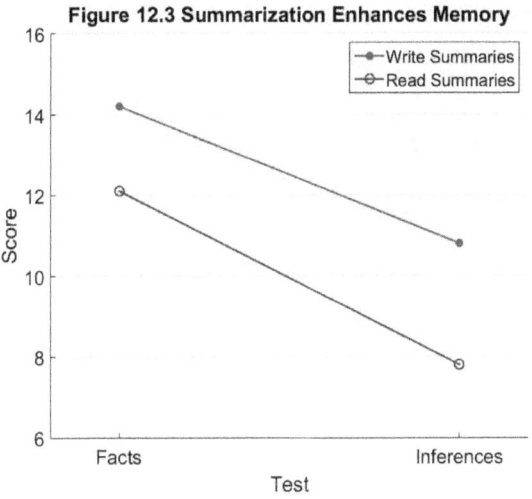

Figure 12.3 Summarization Enhances Memory

Questioning, elaborative interrogation, and self-explanation

<u>While learning a material, simply asking "why?" and trying to figure out the answer enhances memory.</u>

Canadian psychologist Michael Pressley let people learn sentences describing a man's behavior, such as: *The hungry man got into the car; The good man ate dinner.* Some people were further asked to explain and answer the question *Why did the man do that?* Others were further asked to read explanations prepared beforehand, such as: *The hungry man got into the car to go to a restaurant; The kind man is willing to help wash the dishes after dinner.*

Next, people took an unexpected test answering questions like *Who got in the car? Who had dinner?*

As shown in Figure 12.4, compared to those who just read the sentences, those who read the explanations correctly answered more questions, while those who were asked to think of explanations came out with the most correct answers.

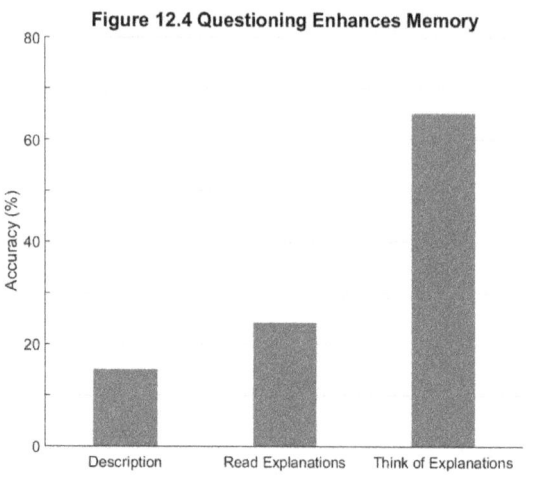

Questioning is similar to the learning technique of elaborative interrogation and self-explanation. During these processes, people either use their previous knowledge and schemas to explain new information or extract related information from the learning material to organize the answer. This requires a high level of semantic processing to make inferences and enhances the systems consolidation of memory.

PART 4
Memory Retrieval and Reconsolidation

CHAPTER 13
The Testing Effect

A curious peculiarity of our memory is that things are impressed better by active than by passive repetition. I mean that in learning (by heart, for example), when we almost know the piece, it pays better to wait and recollect by an effort from within, than to look at the book again. If we recover the words in the former way, we shall probably know them the next time; if in the latter way, we shall very likely need the book once more.

— William James, *Principles of Psychology* (1890)

In 1913, a British elementary school teacher Philip Boswood Ballard noticed something interesting. He asked children to memorize poems, and then tested them several times. Ballard found that lines of the studied poems not recalled on earlier tests could be recalled on later tests despite the absence of new learning (i.e., reviewing).

Sometimes, the total gain compensated forgetting, resulting in overall improved memory performance. Ballard coined the term "reminiscence," referring to the beneficial effect of repeated testing, i.e., memory retrieval, on memory performance.

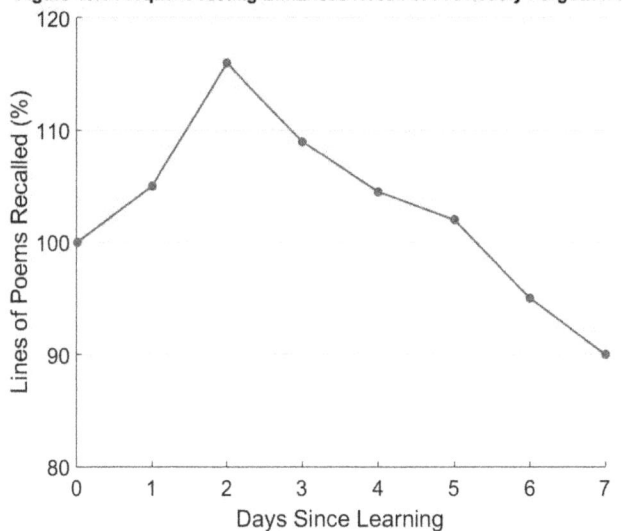

Figure 13.1 Frequent Testing Enhances Recall of Previously Forgotton Items

Almost a century later, Henry L. Roediger III and his student Jeffrey D. Karpicke at Washington University in St. Louis closely studied this phenomenon in the laboratory.

Testing without feedback

In one experiment, Roediger and Karpicke asked college students to read several passages about scientific topics. After reading, half of the students reviewed the contents of the passages again, while the other half received a free recall test without any review.

Students took free recall tests three times: 5 minutes later, on the second day, and one week later. It is important to note that after all tests, none of the students received feedback about their answers. Neither did they have the opportunity to further study the original passages. The result of the tests is shown below.

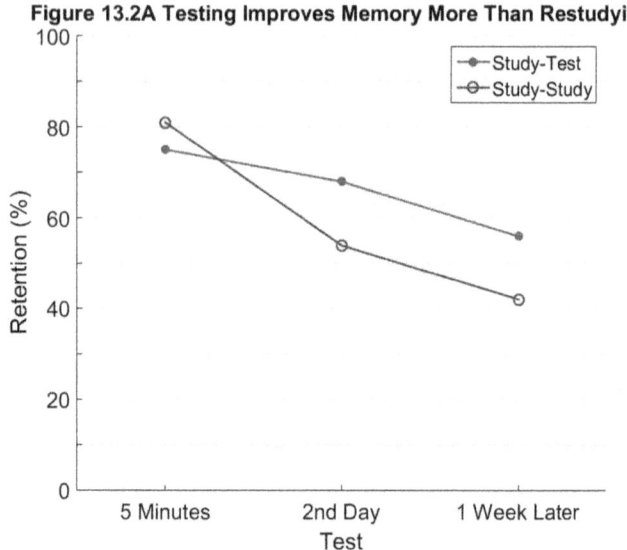

Figure 13.2A Testing Improves Memory More Than Restudying

Although the Study-Study group recalled more contents than the Study-Test group at the immediate test 5 minutes later, it was the Study-Test group that recalled more contents in the tests on the second day and one week later.

Roediger and Karpicke then did another experiment and increased the sessions of tests. They assigned students randomly to one of three groups: Study-Study-Study-Study group; Study-Study-Study-Test group; and Study-Test-

Test-Test group. Those in the first group studied the learning material four times in a row; those in the second group studied three times and received one free recall test; those in the last group studied only once and received three free recall tests.

After that, all students then took a free recall test twice, once 5 minutes later and once 1 week later. Again, no feedback was available after each test. The result is shown below.

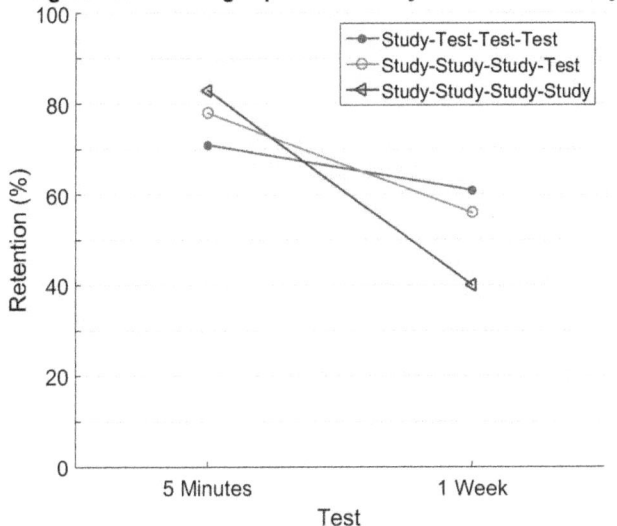

Figure 13.2B Testing Improves Memory More Than Restudying

In the immediate test 5 minutes later, the college students who studied only once but received three tests recalled the least information. However, 1 week later, these students recalled the greatest amount. Notably, the recall in the Study-Test-Test-Test group was about 16 % points higher than the Study-Study-Study-Study group.

<u>Repeated testing strengthens memory more than repeated learning, even when no feedback is provided after each test.</u>

This is known as the Testing Effect. The underlying mechanisms are three-fold. First, testing or memory retrieval activates the memory reconsolidation process.

Second, the practice of retrieval enhances the memory trace and facilitates the extraction of reliable cues for later retrieval.

Third, the process of retrieval reorganizes previously stored information and leads to deep processing. The newly organized information becomes easier to recall. This explains the 1913 observation by Ballard that frequent testing enhances recall of previously forgotten items, despite the absence of subsequent learning.

In line with these mechanisms, compared to multiple-choice tests, short answer tests are more demanding but enhance long-term memory to a greater extent.

Then what happens when feedback is provided after each testing? Will the memory-enhancing effect become bigger?

Testing with feedback

The research team of Henry L. Roediger III and Jeffrey D. Karpicke selected 60 questions from the encyclopedia and presented to their subjects. Examples of the questions included *what is the longest river in the world* (the Nile).

After learning, one third of the subjects received a test (in the form of multiple-choice questions) that covered 40 questions with no feedback, one third received the same test with feedback (they were shown the questions again and the correct answer), while the remaining one third received no test.

On a later test that included all 60 questions, those who took a test with feedback scored over twice as high as those who took a test without feedback and over 3.5 times higher than those who did not take any test.

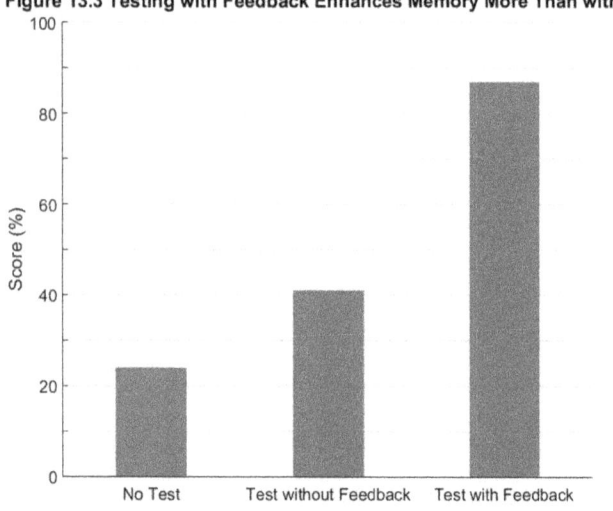

Figure 13.3 Testing with Feedback Enhances Memory More Than without

<u>Restudying after quizzing and getting feedback is referred to as successive relearning. Since testing enhances later encoding of the previously forgotten information, this is also called test-potentiated learning.</u>

Katherine A. Rawson at Kent State University studied the effect of successive relearning with college students enrolled in an Introductory Psychology course. The course covered basic psychological concepts such as classical and instrumental conditioning, memory encoding and retrieval, thinking and intelligence, and cognitive and emotional development. It consisted of 14 lessons delivered in about two months.

After each lesson, half of the students were asked to repeatedly study the concepts as many times as they liked. The other half were told to first try to recall the concepts before restudying them. Therefore, the former group was a repeated learning group, while the latter being successive relearning.

After completing the course, the students took a test and answered questions about the concepts learned. In addition, they took a cued recall test again 3 and 24 days later, during which they had to explain the concepts after being presented certain nouns. It was found those in the successive relearning group consistently outperformed those in the repeated learning group. The difference became more evident on the tests 3 and 24 days later.

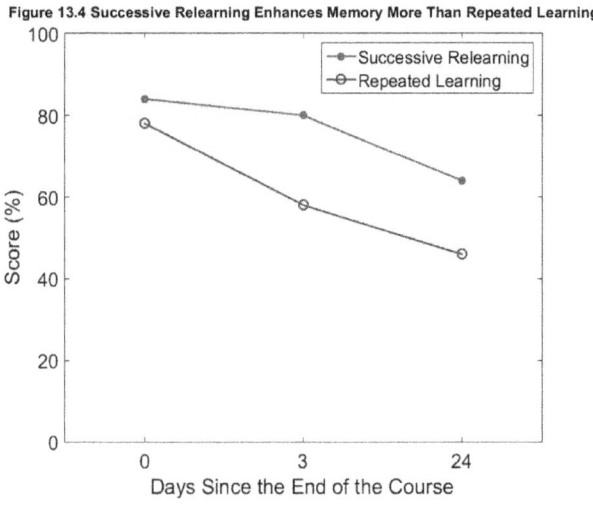

Figure 13.4 Successive Relearning Enhances Memory More Than Repeated Learning

Already mastered knowledge is better repeatedly tested

In another study, Katherine A. Rawson asked English native speakers to learn Swahili-English word pairs. After that, for half of the word pairs, people took three test-restudy sessions: the Swahili word first appeared on the screen and people had to type the English translation; a few seconds later, the correct Swahili-English word pair appeared on the screen so people had the chance to get feedback and relearn. All items repeatedly occurred in the three sessions, whether or not they were correctly recalled. This was the Test-Restudy Fixed condition.

For the other half word pairs, people did three test-restudy sessions under a dropout schedule. Items, once correctly recalled, were eliminated in later sessions. Only the incorrectly answered word pairs were included in the next round of test-restudy session. This is similar to many of our daily life practices where we only review what we have not learned, but stop studying what we have remembered. The test-restudy process repeated until people could correctly answer all the word pairs or they had done 72 test-restudy sessions on a word pair. This was the Test-Restudy Dropout condition.

The Testing Effect

A week later, people received a final test and the result is shown in the following figure. It turned out that the sooner a word was eliminated from the test-restudy session, the worse people's memory of it became in the final test.

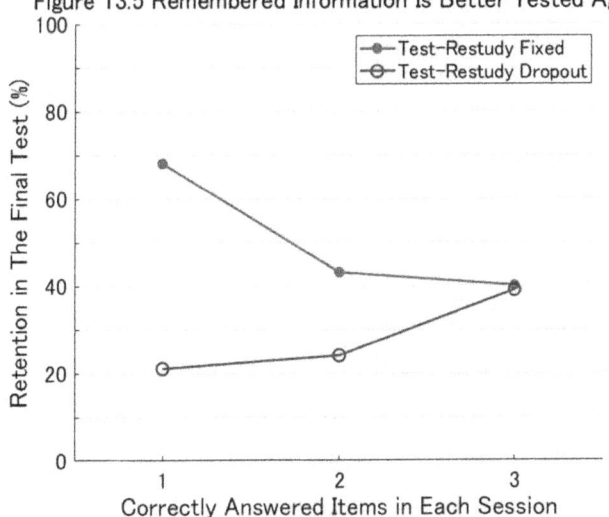

Figure 13.5 Remembered Information Is Better Tested Again

Although repeatedly testing and studying only what one has not remembered is a common practice and saves time, the long-term outcome of this strategy is not ideal. Without repeated testing, people eventually forget what they have learned earlier.

For information that has been mastered, even if you no longer restudy it, it is better repeatedly tested. This helps maintain your memory.

Chapter 14
Memory Retrieval Is a Cue-guided Search Process

There is good evidence that linking words in a story makes them more memorable, but creating your own story, doing your own organizing, leads to even better recall.

— Alan Baddeley, *Essentials of Human Memory*. Classic edition. (2014)

The Search of Associative Memory theory provides a useful model and paradigm for the study of memory retrieval. It was developed by Richard Shiffrin at Indiana University and Jeroen G.W. Raaijmakers at the University of Amsterdam in the Netherlands in the 1980s and has been further revised in 1997 and 2006.

According to this theory, the process of memory retrieval is considered an associative search of the long-term memory guided by cues.

During memory encoding and storage, information is stored as a memory representation or trace. After each learning experience, new memory traces are created.

Memory Retrieval Is a Cue-guided Search Process

Each memory trace contains three parts: the information itself, associative information, and contextual information (such as the episodic information). Each part has distinct features such as color, shape, size and so on. These features are the cues for future recall.

<u>Whether a piece of stored information can be recalled later depends mainly on two factors: the memory strength of the information and the size of the memory search set.</u>

The memory strength of the information is the strength of the association between the available cues and the memory of the information itself. The greater the memory strength of the information, the easier it is retrieved. In general, as time passes, the memory strength of information becomes weaker. This results from two forgetting processes, one passive (natural decay because of molecular turnover) and the other active (which is known as intrinsic forgetting and caused by "forgetting cells" that slowly degrade molecular and cellular memory traces).

The size of the memory search set is determined by the strength of the association between the available cues and other information. The greater the strength of the association between the cues and other information, the bigger the size of the set of memory search, the longer it takes and more difficult it becomes to retrieve the information.

<u>When the association between the cues and the information itself is very strong, and the association between the cues and other information is very weak (or the cues are only associated with little other information), the information can be effectively extracted.</u>

Consistent with this theory, free recall tests provide a more impoverished retrieval environment than cued recall tasks, which, in turn, provide less information about the target memory than a recognition test.

Finding effective cues is the key to successful retrieval

The Dutch psychologist Willem Wagenaar studied the autobiographical memory of himself. For 6 years, between 1978 and 1984, he kept a diary of one or two of the most important events that happened to him every day. For each event, he recorded the time (when), place (where), person (whom), and content (what), each on a separate card. In total, over 2,400 events were recorded.

As an example, on September 10, 1983, Saturday, Wagenaar watched "Last Supper" in a church in Milan with two other psychologists, Elizabeth F. Loftus and James T. Reason.

In 1984, Wagenaar started to test himself to see how much of those events he could recall. Every six months, he tried to use different combinations of the cues (*when*, *where*, *whom*, and *what*) to recall the other information.

For instance, for event A, he tried to start from a cue such as *when* to recall the other three pieces of information, *where*, *whom*, and *what*. For event B, he tried to start from two cues of *where* and *whom* to recall the other information of *when* and *what*. All events were only recalled once. The result of his retrieval is shown in Figure 14.1.

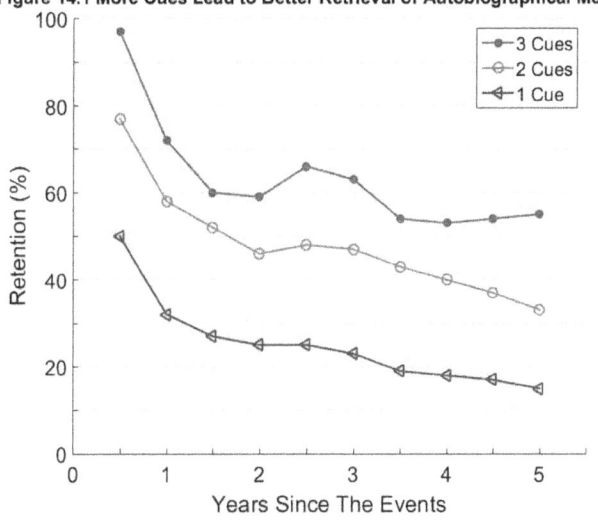

Figure 14.1 More Cues Lead to Better Retrieval of Autobiographical Memory

The memory trajectories generally comply with a typical forgetting curve. Notably, across the five years, more cues consistently led to more information that could be accurately recalled.

<u>More cues lead to better recall.</u>

Meanwhile, Wagenaar noticed that he completely forgot about 20% of the events that had happened 5 years ago, even after reading all the cues. Does that mean all those memories have been lost and can never be recovered?

Wagenaar was curious about the answer to this question, so he met with the other persons involved in 10 forgotten events to see if they could provide any specific details.

Interestingly, with the help of those people, Wagenaar could remember all the details of those 10 events. He concluded that "…in light of this one cannot say that any event was completely forgotten."

Wagenaar's finding was confirmed in the laboratory by Swedish psychologist Timo Mäntylä at Umeå University. Mäntylä asked people to learn over 500 randomly selected nouns. For each noun, they had to think of either 1 or 3 words to describe it. For instance, in the case of "tree," people could think of "high," or "high, green, and umbrella." In the later recall test, these subjects-generated words were used as cues for the retrieval of the original nouns.

As shown in Figure 14.2, 3 cues continuously brought a higher recall than 1 cue, whether the test was delivered immediately, or 1, 2, or 7 days after the initial learning session.

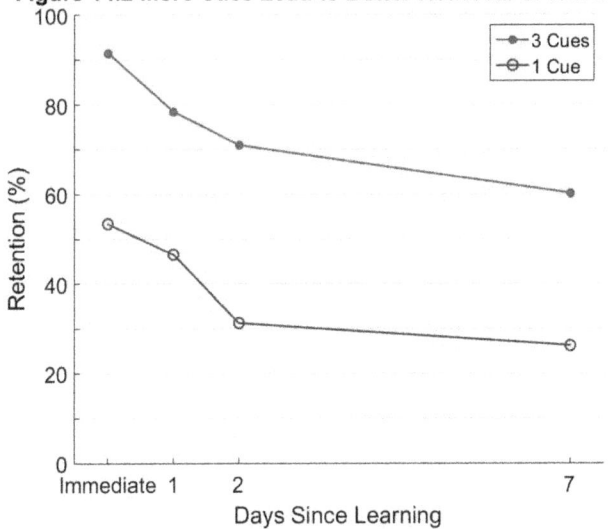

Figure 14.2 More Cues Lead to Better Retrieval of Word Lists

To some extent, forgetting is but our inability to retrieve specific information given limited cues.

Chapter 15
The Context of Memory

I think I'm really good at forgetting about golf when I'm off the golf course.

— Inbee Park, Former No. 1 Ranked Player in the Women's World Golf Ranking

An American stayed in China for several years and eventually could speak Chinese fluently. However, a few years after his return to the U.S., he found himself unable to speak and understand Chinese anymore. He expected that when he returned to China, he would have to use much effort to relearn the language. To his surprise, upon his return to China, he was able to speak the language as fluently as before.

Environmental contexts

Inspired by similar phenomena, two British psychologists, Duncan Godden and Alan Baddeley, speculated that perhaps environmental cues are important in helping people access relevant memories. They then set up an experiment to test this hypothesis.

They asked divers to listen to 40 unrelated words in two different environments: on dry land and underwater.

Later they tested the divers in either the same or an alternative environment of the initial learning.

<u>Interestingly, words learned on land were better recalled on land, while words learned underwater were better recalled underwater.</u>

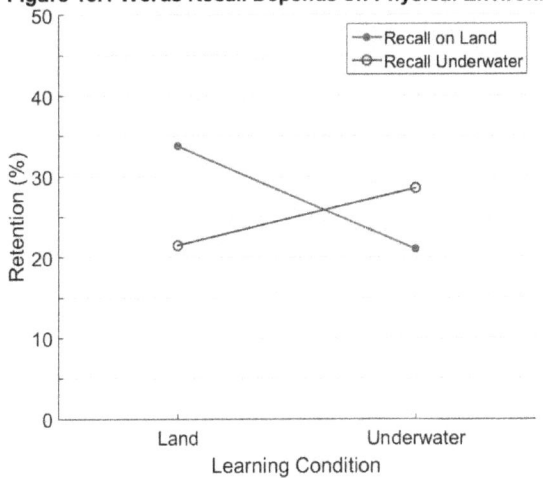

Figure 15.1 Words Recall Depends on Physical Environment

Similarly, in another study by Steven M. Smith at Texas A&M University, the recall of words was found to depend on the background music. Subjects learned vocabularies while listening to Mozart's piano concerto or jazz. Immediately after learning and two days later, they were asked to recall all the words while listening to Mozart's piano concerto, jazz, or in a quiet environment. Both tests indicated a background-dependent effect: words learned under Mozart were better recalled under Mozart compared to jazz or in quiet; words learned under jazz were better recalled under jazz compared to Mozart or in quiet.

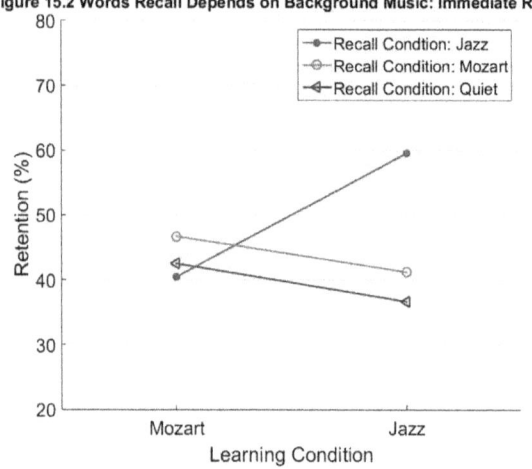

Figure 15.2 Words Recall Depends on Background Music: Immediate Recall

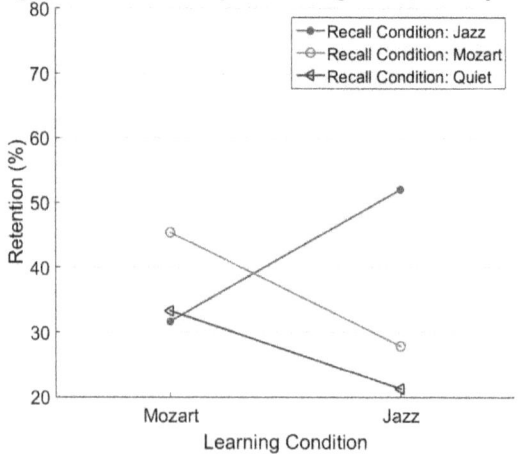

Figure 15.3 Words Recall Depends on Background Music: Delayed Recall

<u>The environmental context serves as a cue for memory retrieval.</u>

Internal states

Besides external environmental context, the internal context or state also affects memory. Heavy drinkers often find that while sober, they cannot remember where they have hidden alcohol or money when drunk; when they become drunk again, they remember. Donald W. Goodwin and colleagues at Washington University confirmed this phenomenon in the laboratory:

<u>What is learned when drunk is better recalled while drunk.</u>

Another kind of internal state is mood. Mood-congruent memory is a well-established phenomenon. When in a positive mood, people are more likely to recall happy memories; when in a negative mood, people are more likely to recall bad memories. Emotion or mood itself serves as a cue for memory retrieval. Meanwhile, it is also observed that information learned under a certain mood is better recalled under that same mood.

Although sometimes people may use the context-dependent feature of memory to enhance recall—for instance, actors remember scripts by vividly imagining the feelings of the character associated with the scripts—usually we want the memories to persist in different contexts. Therefore, strategies to reduce the influence by the context of the initial learning are important.

Strategies to reduce context-dependent forgetting

Three strategies prove effective. First, use deep processing or elaborative encoding strategies during learning, such as linking information with one's prior knowledge. This suppresses the influence of contextual cues and increases the strength of the memory information.

Second, vary the conditions of learning to remove the influence of the context-dependent memory.

<u>If knowledge is repeatedly learned, extracted, and used in different contexts, it can be decontextualized. Varying the context of learning can reduce the memory strength of contextual cues and enhance that of other, meaningful cues such as semantic links and schemas.</u>

For instance, in one study, Steven M. Smith found that studying the same material in two rooms resulted in better recall compared to studying twice in the same room.

Figure 15.4 Varying Learning Contexts Enhances Memory

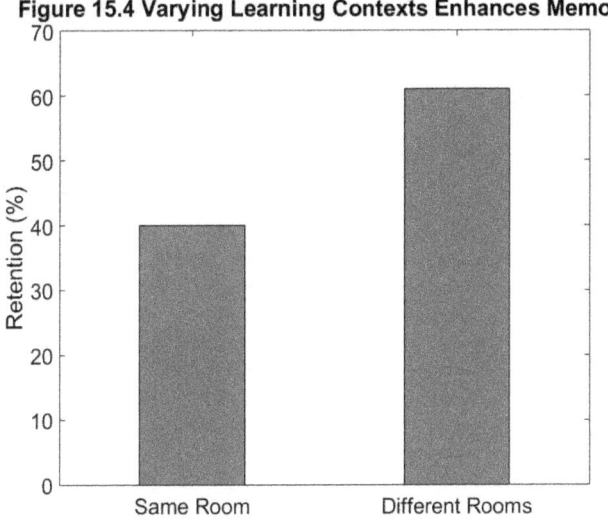

Therefore, instead of always studying in your office or classroom, try various places sometimes. The library, meeting room, and a quiet coffee shop are all good choices. And each time, sit in a different seat as this further helps decontextualize your learning.

In addition, the Spacing Effect (see Chapter 16)—distributed learning separated apart in time is better than massed learning in rapid succession—is partially based on this mechanism.

Third, try to recall the initial context. Mental imagination of the initial context of learning helps activate the memory of the stored information.

In one study, Steven M. Smith asked subjects to learn word lists in one room and then tested them in another room. At the test, half of the subjects first recalled the context of the initial room and listed three objects in that room.

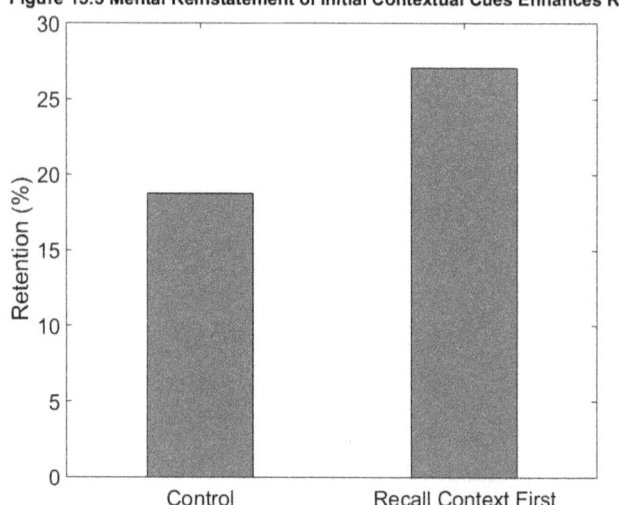

Figure 15.5 Mental Reinstatement of Initial Contextual Cues Enhances Recall

As shown in Figure 15.5, this simple mental reinstatement of the initial contextual cues improved their remembered words by over 8%.

CHAPTER 16
Spaced Learning

The [person] who works so moderately as to be able to work constantly, not only preserves his [or her] health the longest, but in the course of the year, executes the greatest quantity of work.

— Adam Smith, *The Wealth of Nations* (1776)

In Chapter 1 we introduced the 50-year-long forgetting curve of a foreign language Spanish reported by psychologist Harry P. Bahrick. In his study, Bahrick observed another phenomenon:

<u>Compared to massed practice in rapid succession, distributed or spaced practice separated apart in time enhances memory.</u>

Bahrick asked subjects to learn Spanish words using a test-study procedure. Each session, subjects received a test, after which they only studied what they answered incorrectly.

The first group of subjects served as the control group, and only attended one session of training. The second to fourth group attended 6–8 sessions. Specifically, the second group finished all the sessions on the same day.

The third group did one session each day and needed 6–8 days to finish all the training. The fourth group did one session every 30 days and needed 6–8 months to finish all the training.

Whereas the second group was a typical mass learning or intensive practice, the third and fourth groups were considered spaced learning.

It was insured that after all the training, people had no chance to learn these word pairs in their daily life. About 6–9 years later, Bahrick tested all the subjects' memory of the word pairs. The tests included a free recall test and a recognition test. In the free recall test, people had to answer the corresponding Spanish word after seeing an English word. Those Spanish words that people could not recall were mixed with a couple of new words for people to identify in the recognition test.

As shown in Figure 16.1A, compared to the control group who attended only 1 session of training, the other groups who attended 6–8 sessions had better recognition and free recall memory. Among those who attended 6–8 sessions, those who split each session every 30 days had the best memory, followed by those who did one session each day. In other words, spaced learning enhances memory more than massed learning.

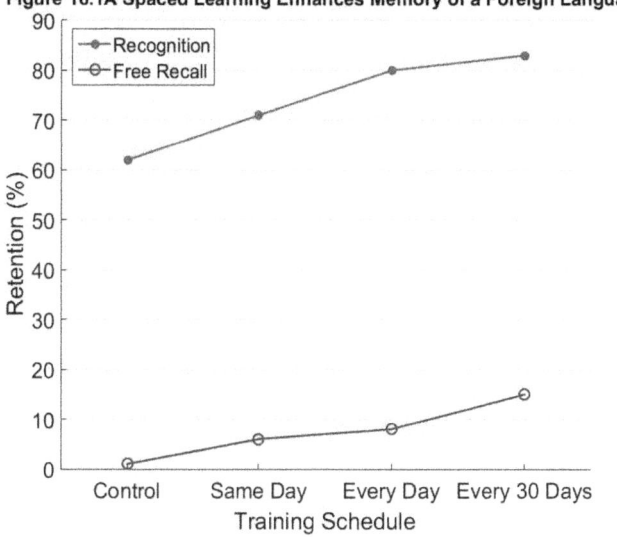

Figure 16.1A Spaced Learning Enhances Memory of a Foreign Language

Using the same method, Bahrick asked subjects to learn English-French or English-German word pairs. Subjects had either 13 or 26 sessions of training, which were spread every 14, 28, or 56 days. So for those with 26 sessions every 56 days, they took over 4 years to finish all the training.

Bahrick then tested the subjects' memory at 1, 2, 3, and 5 years after their last training session. To his surprise, those who split learning for a longer period had better memory throughout the 5 years after training, as shown in Figure 16.1B.

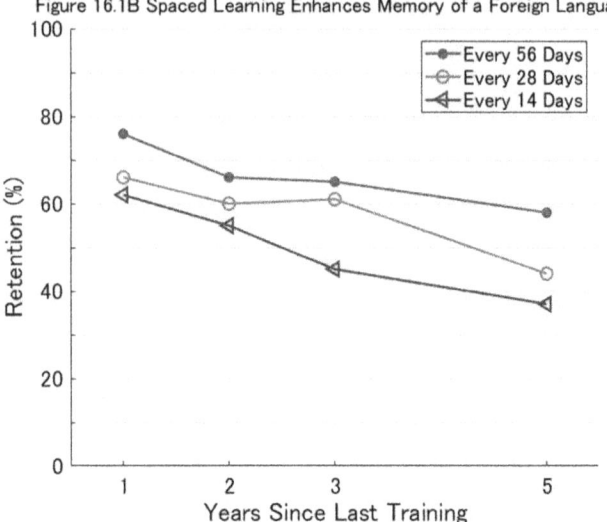

Figure 16.1B Spaced Learning Enhances Memory of a Foreign Language

This was true whether subjects practiced 13 or 26 sessions (Figure 16.1C). Remarkably, subjects who practiced 13 sessions spaced at every 56 days performed better than those who practiced 26 sessions spaced at every 14 days.

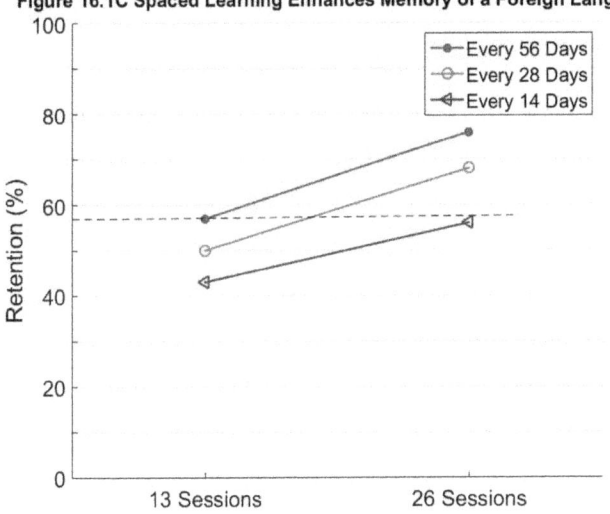

Figure 16.1C Spaced Learning Enhances Memory of a Foreign Language

In real life classrooms, Canadian psychologist Nicholas J. Cepeda at York University let 10-year-old primary school students learn the definition of unfamiliar English words. Half of them reviewed the words for a second time 10 minutes later, while the other half 1 week later. In a test delivered 5 weeks later, those who learned at intervals of 10 minutes correctly recalled 7.5% of all the words. In sharp contrast, those who learned at intervals of 1 week correctly recalled almost three times more: 20.8%.

Nicholas J. Cepeda performed a systematic review in 2006 and identified 839 studies that compared the learning effects of spaced/distributed vs massed practice. Cepeda concluded that:

<u>Spaced practice enhances memory more than the same amount of massed practice.</u>

But the optimal intervals of each practice vary according to the test interval.

<u>As the test interval becomes longer, the optimal interval of each practice also increases.</u>

Cepeda further conducted an experiment to identify the optimal interval of each practice. Cepeda let over 1,350 subjects learn 32 sets of facts, such as *which European country eats the spiciest Mexican food?* (The answer is Norway). There were two learning sessions scattered to different time intervals.

For both learning sessions, people used the test-study procedure. In the first session, people repeated the procedure until they learned all the facts. In the second session, they did only two test-study processes. The intervals between the two sessions varied between 1 day to 3.5 months. People received tests at different intervals of 7, 35, 70, and 350 days following the final learning.

The optimal interval for spaced learning according to different test intervals is presented in Table 16.1.

Table 16.1 Optimal Learning Intervals According to Test Intervals

	Free Recall Test		**Recognition Test**	
Test interval	Optimal learning interval	Memory improved	Optimal learning interval	Memory improved
7 days	3 days	10%	1.6 days	1%
35 days	8 days	59%	7 days	10%
70 days	12 days	111%	10 days	31%
350 days	27 days	77%	25 days	60%

As can be seen, for tests 1 week later, the optimal learning interval is 2–3 days; for tests 1 months later, around 1 week; 2 months later, around 10 days; 1 year later, around 1 month.

These are the optimal learning interval for just two learning sessions and may not apply to many real life situations where we study the same material several times. But these findings suggest that to promote long-term memory, it is recommended to review information after a period of spaced interval rather than immediately in rapid succession.

Fixed vs extended spacing

There are two types of spacing. In fixed spacing, the spacing gaps between each learning session are identical. For instance, we learn a text 4 times, each separated by 2 weeks. So in a total of 6 weeks, learning is spaced by a 2-2-2 (week) schedule.

In extended spacing, the spacing gap between the learning sessions becomes longer. To learn a text 4 times, we study it the second time 1 week later, the third time 2 weeks later, and the fourth time 3 weeks later. In 6 weeks, learning is spaced by a 1-2-3 (week) schedule.

Research shows that for the same length of study period (in the above example, 6 weeks) and the same number of sessions (in the above example, 3 sessions), the two types of spacing create similar learning results better than massed practice.

Why spaced learning is better than massed learning

First, after each learning, there is a memory consolidation process, which takes days, weeks, to months. Generally, longer intervals between learning sessions allow more memory consolidation to complete.

Second, as the interval between learning sessions increases, the memory consolidation process becomes more complete, so the next session of learning acts like testing and reactivates the memory. This triggers reconsolidation.

Third, during spaced practice, people generally pay more attention to the learning material. Compared to massed practice, people feel less familiar with or even "forget" the learning material and therefore are more likely to invest much effort in encoding during spaced practice.

Fourth, spaced learning brings diversity to the encoding context. This reduces context-dependent forgetting and strengthens the association between semantic cues and the memory information itself.

CHAPTER 17
Interleaved Learning

Interleaved learning is related to but slightly different from spaced learning. Spaced learning generally focuses on the same learning material, while interleaved learning emphasizes the practice of different materials. The counterpart of spaced learning is massed learning, while the counterpart of interleaved learning is blocked learning.

A study conducted by Doug Rohrer and Kelli Taylor at the University of South Florida provided an excellent example of the superior memory effect of interleaved over blocked learning.

Taylor and Rohrer asked college students to learn to compute the volumes of 4 geometric solids. Half of the students were assigned to the blocked practice group and practiced four questions for each solid in turn (i.e., aaaabbbbccccdddd). The other half of the students were assigned to the interleaved practice group and practiced one question for each solid and repeated this process four times (i.e., abcdabcdabcdabcd).

One week later, they did another practice session like this. And two weeks later, they received a test and answered two new questions for each solid.

As shown in Figure 17.1, although during the practice session, the blocked practice group scored about 30% points higher, their performance dropped substantially in the test session. In contrast, the interleaved practice group maintained their accuracy. As a result, the interleaved practice group scored over 40% points higher than the blocked practice group.

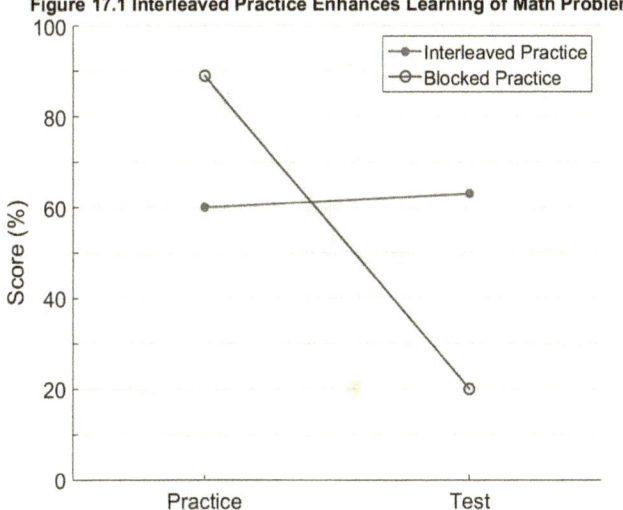

Figure 17.1 Interleaved Practice Enhances Learning of Math Problems

<u>Interleaved learning or mixing multiple types of materials enhances memory more than blocked learning or repeatedly studying a single type of material before moving to the next.</u>

In another study, Nate Kornell and Robert A. Bjork at UCLA let people study multiple paintings by different, unknown artists. For half of the paintings, subjects studied a given artist's paintings consecutively before going on to another artist's paintings (blocked). For the other half, all the artists' paintings were mixed and subjects studied the paintings in an interleaved manner. Later, subjects were presented 4 new paintings of each artist and had to judge which belonged to whom.

As can be seen from Figure 17.2, compared to blocked practice, interleaved practice led to an over 25% higher accuracy.

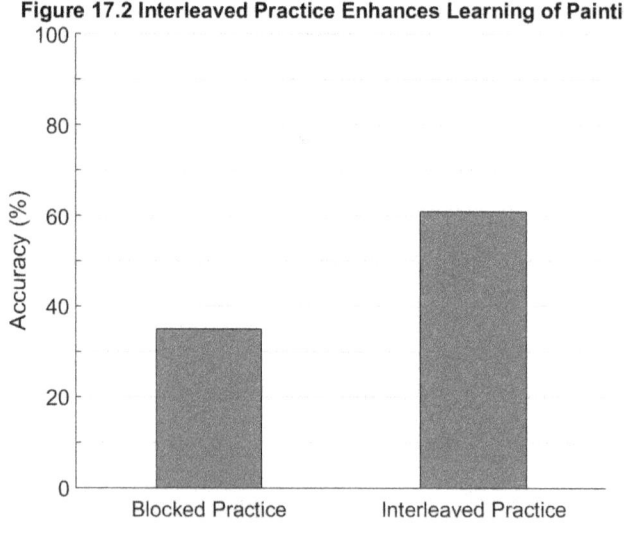

Figure 17.2 Interleaved Practice Enhances Learning of Paintings

Similarly, in a third study by Geoffrey R. Norman at McMaster University, Canada, medical students learned to diagnose three heart diseases based on ECG. Half of the students were assigned to a blocked practice group and studied four examples in a row after each disease. The other half students were assigned to an interleaved practice group and randomly studied the examples of each disease.

When later asked to diagnose new examples, students in the interleaved practice group outperformed those in the blocked practice group by almost 20% in accuracy.

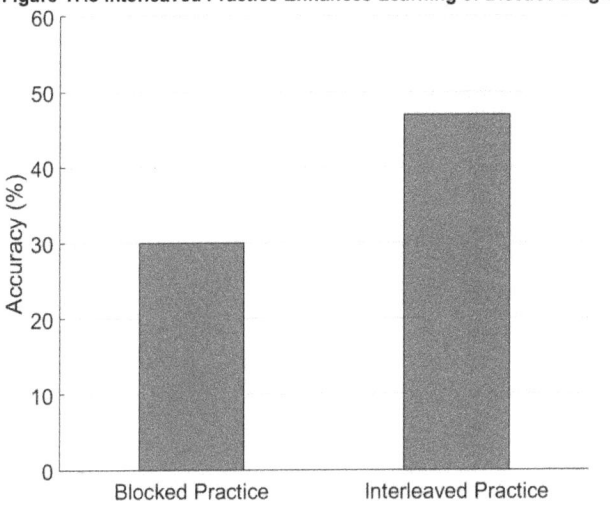

Figure 17.3 Interleaved Practice Enhances Learning of Disease Diagnosis

Why is interleaved practice better than blocked practice?

First, like spaced learning, interleaved practice allows the memory consolidation process to complete to a greater extent.

Second, during interleaved practice, people must switch between different tasks many times, and this helps distinguish between the various tasks/categories and identify similarities within the same category.

Third, interleaved practice reduces "memory fatigue" because of repeated learning of the same material. It facilitates the release from proactive interference, which is the content of the next chapter.

CHAPTER 18
What Causes Forgetting: Memory Interference

According to the traditional theory, the forgetting of memory is mainly caused by the passage of time. Over time, memory traces fade and disappear. However, as we have shown earlier, memory is usually quite stable and as long as we can find effective cues, we can access much of them. Therefore, forgetting has been defined as the inability to retrieve specific information given limited cues.

Here, we consider the following question:

<u>Why can't limited cues activate the stored memory of a specific piece of information?</u>

<u>According to the memory retrieval theory, that is because the limited cues have also been associated with other information and are not specific enough to activate the target information. During this process, a mutual interference occurs. The newly stored memory and the old memory interfere with each other.</u>

There are two basic interferences: retroactive interference and proactive interference.

Retroactive interference

<u>Retroactive interference occurs when new information interferes with or somehow supersedes the old, previously learned information.</u>

As one example, psychologists asked subjects to learn several lists of adjectives and found that forgetting was the least when subjects simply rested during the interval between learning and testing. When they learned other adjectives—particularly those with similar meanings to the initially learned—before testing, forgetting of the initially learned adjectives increased.

In another study, subjects first read an article about 200 words describing a person's childhood experience and received a test of the contents. Half of the subjects then read another article about the child experience of two other people (Similar Information), while the other half read an article about an island and a library (Different Information). Later, they received a test about the first article, the result of which is shown in Figure 18.1.

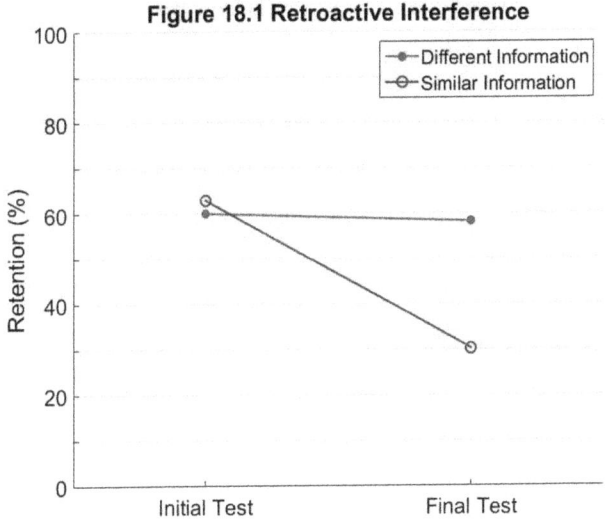

Figure 18.1 Retroactive Interference

Although subjects initially remembered the first article to a similar degree, those who subsequently read similar information demonstrated reduced memory of the first article.

<u>Learning similar information reduces the memory of previously learned information.</u>

Cued recall reduces retroactive interference

In a study by Canadian psychologist Endel Tulving, people learned 6 word lists. Each list contained 24 words and every 4 words belonged to a category (such as animals). Following that, people took an immediate free recall test and a delayed free recall test after another irrelevant control task.

In both tests, all subjects showed the retroactive interference effect: earlier lists were remembered worse than later lists.

Then they received another cued recall test. The category names of the words were presented to them as the cues for recall. This time, as shown in Figure 19.2, the retroactive interference effect disappeared: subjects could recall all lists equally well, irrespective of the order.

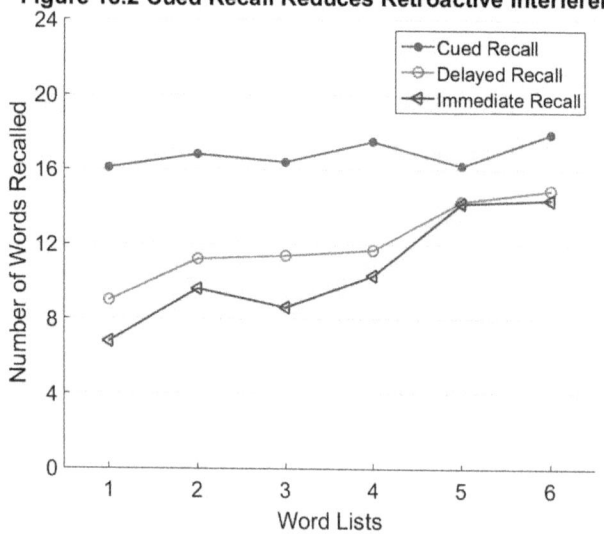

Figure 18.2 Cued Recall Reduces Retroactive Interference

<u>Using specific cues to recall information reduces retroactive interference.</u>

One more example of this is the use of mnemonics such as the peg-word system, which will be introduced in Chapter 23.

Proactive interference

<u>Proactive interference is when an old memory interferes with the learning of new information.</u>

British psychologist Barrie Gunter at the University of Leicester let subjects read either four political news articles (such as diplomatic news) or four industrial news articles (such as a report about a professional manager) in a row. Immediately after each article, subjects took a test. After the last test following the last article, people received a final, delayed test of all the articles. Gunter found that in both the immediate and delayed test, people showed a proactive interference effect: their memory of more recent articles declined (see Figure 18.3, Same Topic).

<u>Repeatedly learning the same material in a row reduces memory performance.</u>

However, when Gunter asked another group of subjects to first read three political articles and then one industrial article, or three industrial articles followed by a political article, people's memory of the last article improved. The proactive interference effect disappeared (see Figure 18.3, Last Topic Changed). This is called "release from proactive interference."

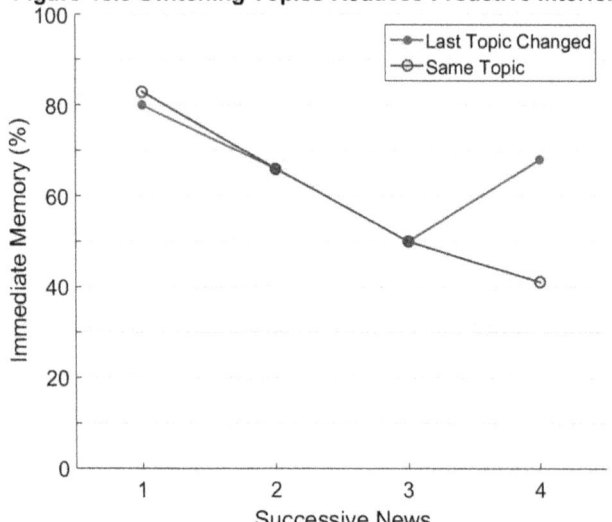

Figure 18.3 Switching Topics Reduces Proactive Interference

This supports the superior memory effect of interleaved learning.

<u>Changing the topics or categories of material resets the memory performance.</u>

<u>Similarly, changing the encoding mode such as from visual to auditory also promotes the release from proactive interference.</u>

Testing reduces retroactive and proactive interferences

Psychologist Katherine A. Rawson at Washington University in St. Louis found that:

<u>An interim test can reduce proactive interference.</u>

Rawson let people study three articles on greenhouse gas. One group studied all three articles in a row. A second group underwent an interim recall test after the first two articles. A third group solved some math problems after the first two articles. After studying the third article, everyone received a free recall test on the third article.

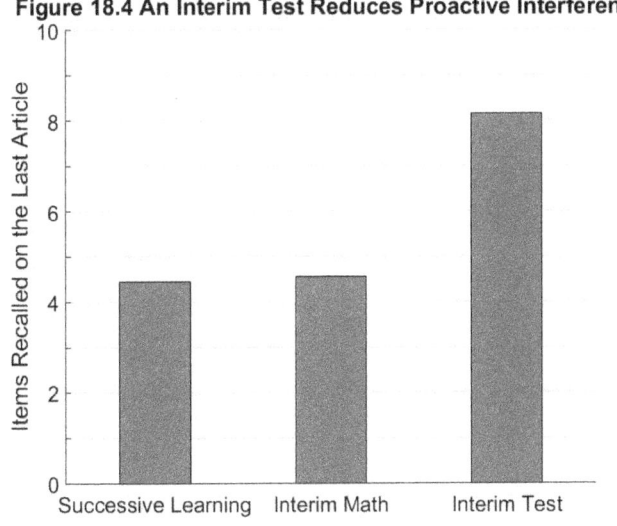

Figure 18.4 An Interim Test Reduces Proactive Interference

Whereas solving math problems did not improve recall of the last article, an interim test dramatically increased recall. Therefore, testing previous learning facilitates subsequent learning of new information.

Testing also reduces retroactive interference.

Rosalind Potts and David R. Shanks at University College London asked native English speakers to learn Swahili-English word pairs. After that, half of the subjects then learned Finnish-English word pairs. Understandably, Finnish interfered with Swahili because they shared the same English cues. On the second day of testing, it was found that those who learned the additional Finnish-English word pairs performed worse on the recall of the Swahili words.

Interestingly, in a later experiment, when the psychologists asked half of the subjects to receive a test of the Swahili-English word pairs before they learned the Finnish-English word pairs, the interference effect of Finnish on Swahili disappeared.

Therefore, testing is an effective strategy to reduce both retroactive and proactive interferences.

CHAPTER 19
Memory Retrieval Is a Reconstruction Process: The Side Effect of Schemas

An organism has somehow to acquire the capacity to turn round upon its own "schemata" and to construct them afresh.

— Frederick C. Bartlett, *Remembering* (1932)

In 1932, British psychologist Frederick C. Bartlett proposed the concept of *reconstructive memory* in his book *Remembering: a study in experimental and social psychology*.

Bartlett argued that most people do not remember exactly what has happened to them. When they recall information, they reconstruct their memory in a way that complies with previous personal experience and knowledge, or schemas.

Bartlett asked English subjects to read several folk stories about North American Indians. One was *The War of the Ghosts*, with some supernatural elements such as *When the sun rose he fell down. Something black came out of his mouth.* This seemed bizarre to the highly educated English subjects.

Bartlett found that when asked to recall the stories later, these subjects reconstructed the stories from their own perspectives. The retold stories were always shorter, more coherent, and conformed to typical European expectations. Bartlett identified three patterns of errors that occurred during the reconstruction process.

First, unusual or strange items are likely to be omitted. Second, unfamiliar names or terms are changed to familiar ones (e.g., *canoes* become *boats*). Third, rationalizations—making up reasons—occur to explain the phenomena and make the stories more coherent (e.g., *the Ghosts* becomes the name of a clan; s*omething black came out of his mouth* becomes *foamed at the mouth*).

Schemas allow fast systems consolidation and enhance memory. However, sometimes they introduce errors into our memory, as the process of memory retrieval is guided by schemas.

Schemas or perspectives affect memory and retrieval

<u>For the same event, different people have different interpretations and memories.</u>

This is well illustrated by a classic study published in the 1950s by social psychologists Albert H. Hastorf at

Dartmouth College and Hadley Cantril at Princeton University.

Following a very violent college football game between Dartmouth and Princeton, students in these two colleges rated the violations made by the opposing team more flagrant than those made by their own.

<u>Switching perspectives or schemas often facilitates memory.</u>

In a study conducted by Richard C. Anderson and James W. Pichert at the University of Illinois, subjects read a story about two boys skipping school and visiting another boy's home. But while reading, subjects had to take the perspective of either a burglar or a person interested in buying a home. Later, all subjects were asked to recall the story twice in a row, but for the second recall, they had to change their perspective.

It was found that compared to the first recall, during the second recall, the subjects mentioned more details important to the other perspective they did not recall earlier. Thus, "burglars" recalled more information about the "loot," while the "home buyers" were more concerned with the number of rooms and the leaky ceiling.

Inference reconstruction

One mechanism by which schemas bring wrong memory is inference. For instance, browse the following two word lists:

A. bed, rest, awake, tired, dream, wake-up, night, doze, pillow

B. apples, vegetables, oranges, bananas, orange juice, cherries, baskets, pears, kiwi

Now, please try to recall each list.

When you finish, please answer the following two questions.

Is "sleep" on list A?

Is "fruit" on list B?

Psychologist Henry L. Roediger III asked people to read similar word lists and found that during a later test, people recalled words such as *sleep* and *fruit* that did not exist in, but were easily inferred from the lists.

Similarly, in another study, John D. Bransford at the State University of New York asked people to read sentences such as *There is a box to the right of a tree* and *There is a chair on the box*. Later, people remembered reading the sentence *The tree is to the left of the chair*, although that sentence was not presented and based on people's inference.

<u>Information not present, but easily inferred by schemas intrudes into the original memory.</u>

The interaction of elaboration and inferential reconstruction

Earlier, we discussed how elaborative encoding enhances memory. Such elaborative encoding facilitates the process of inference and the forming of new schemas. Therefore,

<u>Elaborative encoding leads to both an increased recall of what has been studied and an increase in the number of inferences recalled.</u>

An experiment by Justine Owens and Gordon H. Bower at Stanford University and John B. Black at the University of Illinois confirmed this prediction. Subjects read a story about a college student, which included five life events: making a cup of coffee in the morning, going to see the doctor, visiting a grocery, attending a lecture, and attending a party. The following is a passage from the story:

"Nancy went to the doctor. She arrived at the office and checked in with the receptionist. She went to see the nurse who went through the usual procedures. Then Nancy

stepped on the scale and the nurse recorded her weight. The doctor entered the room and examined the results. He smiled at Nancy and said, 'Well, it seems my expectations have been confirmed.' When the examination was finished, Nancy left the office."

Notably, half of the subjects had read the following background information at the beginning of the experiment:

"Nancy woke up feeling sick again and she wondered if she really were pregnant. How would she tell the professor she had been seeing? And the money was another problem."

The subjects who read this additional background information characterized Nancy as a student afraid of being pregnant because of an affair with her college professor. The other half of the subjects did not read this background information and had no reason to make such inference.

All the subjects were asked to recall the story 24 hours later. As can be seen from Figure 19.1, those who read the background information remembered more inferences not in the original story. For instance, many subjects recalled that the doctor told Nancy she was pregnant. Intrusions of this variety are expected if subjects reconstruct a story based on their inferences.

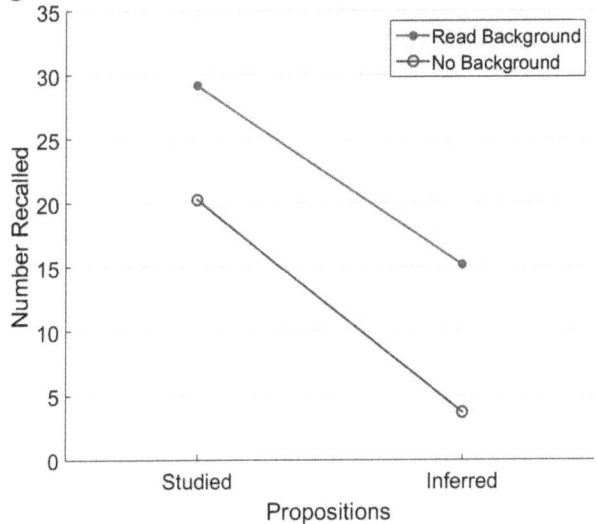

Figure 19.1 The Interaction Between Elaboration and Inference

Meanwhile, subjects who read the background information recalled more propositions that they had actually studied. Because of the additional elaborations during encoding, they could memorize more of the story.

It is perfectly right for people to make inferences and recall them. In non-experimental settings, such as recalling information for an exam, this is helpful.

PART 5
Mnemonics

CHAPTER 20
How Do Mental Athletes Remember Everything?

Professional mnemonists or mental athletes are good at remembering meaningless, random digits, names, and cards. They do this excellent job in typically three steps.

Step 1: coding or converting the to-be-remembered information into words, characters, or images. This creates meaningful material easily remembered.

Step 2: forming vivid mental images. Visual imagery is a powerful mnemonic to memorize meaningful information.

Step 3: chaining the mental images by familiar mediators. These mediators serve as cues for later retrieval.

In this chapter, we introduce the major system for step 1. In Chapter 21, we focus on visual imagery. In Chapter 22 and 23, we introduce two chaining mnemonics, the method of loci and the peg-word system.

The major system

The major system, also called the phonetic number system or phonetic mnemonic system, is specifically used for memorizing numbers, such as phone numbers, credit card numbers, pin codes, postcodes, and birthdays. It works by converting numbers into consonant sounds and then by adding vowels, combining them to form words. Words can further form stories that can be visualized. In this way, numbers are converted into meaningful stories.

There are different versions of the major system, below is one frequently used example.

Table 20.1 The Major System

	Sounds	Letters
0	/s/, /z/	s, z
1	/t/, /d/, (/θ/, /ð/)	t, d, th (in *thing*)
2	/n/	n
3	/m/	m
4	/r/	r
5	/l/	l
6	/tʃ/, /ʃ/, /dʒ/, /ʒ/	ch (in *cheese*), sh (in *shine*), j, soft g, t (in *equation*)
7	/k/	k, hard c, q, ch (in *loch*), hard g
8	/f/, /v/	f, ph (in *phone*), v, gh (in *laugh*)
9	/b/, /p/	b, p

You can use any words, including nouns, verbs, and adjectives, to code digits. Here is a list of nouns coding 0 to 99.

0–9: zoo, tie, hen, home, arrow, law, shoe, cow, ivy, bee

10–19: tooth, date, tin, time, diary, towel, dish, dog, dove, type

20–29: nose, net, nano, name, owner, nail, niche, neck, knife, nap

30–39: mouse, mood, moon, memo, humor, male, match, mug, movie, map

40–49: rice, road, urn, rum, error, railway, roach, rock, roof, rope

50–59: lace, lady, lion, loom, lure, lily, lash, lake, leaf, lip

60–69: cheese, sheet, chain, jam, cherry, July, cha-cha, chick, chef, jeep

70–79: kiss, cat, coin, game, car, coal, cage, cake, cave, cube

80–89: vase, video, phone, foam, fairy, fly, fish, fog, viva, vibe

90–99: boss, bat, bone, puma, berry, bell, beach, bike, beef, baby

To remember long digits, after some practice, you will soon find that words coding 3–4 or even 5 digits are preferred. If you build a pool of codes and memorize them, it is easy to quickly convert digits to words and stories.

As one example, the title of this book "*Strategic Memory: The Natural History of Learning and Forgetting*" is equal to 014167-334-1-2145-014-8-54226-21-847126.

This sequence can also be converted to:

"Sweetheart, she came mere tonight

A royal strawflower in ancient

Very good

Enjoy"

Strawflower is also known as golden everlasting.

<u>The major system works perfectly for memorizing numbers, although the coding requires much effort and practice.</u>

CHAPTER 21
Visual Imagery

One common strategy used by professional mnemonists is visual imagery. It is based on the observation that:

<u>Our memory of concrete, vivid visual stimuli such as pictures is far more stable than other stimuli.</u>

Harvard psychologist Roger N. Shepard asked people to browse over 600 color pictures and later tested their ability to identify the pictures from a pool of mixed pictures. Surprisingly, their memory was quite accurate. The forgetting curve of pictures is similar to that of words and events, but the speed of forgetting is far slower. After 4 months, recognition accuracy is still as high as 60%.

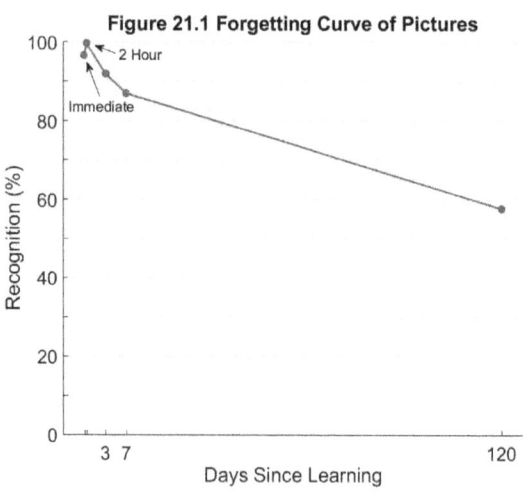

Figure 21.1 Forgetting Curve of Pictures

Why images are better remembered

One explanation is based on the Dual Coding Theory proposed by psychologist Allan Paivio at the University of Western Ontario. According to this theory, compared to words primarily represented by verbal codes (modes), images are more likely to be represented by both verbal and image/visual codes. It is partly supported by the observation that it is easier to name a picture than to form mental images of a word.

As the capacity of each mode is limited, this kind of dual-coding reduces the memory load and extends the processing ability, leaving space for more active encoding. This theory is in line with the Modality Effect (Chapter 8).

Another explanation is the sensory-semantic model proposed by Douglas L. Nelson at the University of South Florida. This theory holds that pictures are more distinct from each other than words. This is consistent with the Distinctiveness Effect (Chapter 6). Indeed, the superior memory effect of pictures disappears as the visual similarity among the pictures increases.

Compared to words, pictures are at a deeper level of processing. This is supported by neuroimaging evidence that compared to words, pictures more effectively and automatically activate brain regions important for visual memory, including the medial temporal cortex. In line with this, more interactive, vivid, concrete mental imagery produces better memory.

Visual imagery

<u>Reading, when combined with vivid mental or visual imagery, can dramatically improve memory.</u>

It is because vivid visual imagery enhances information processing in the visual mode. It is a combination of elaborative encoding and systems consolidation.

Canadian psychologist Michael Pressley asked 3rd grade elementary students to read a story and then tested their memory. For half of the students, Pressley trained them to form vivid, live visual images of the story, for instance, *Kids riding on whales*. While for the other half, Pressley just asked them to remember the content of the story in whatever way they could.

At a later test, students who used visual imagery, irrespective of their reading ability, recalled more contents correctly, as seen in Figure 21.2.

<u>Students poor at reading benefit more from using the visual imagery technique.</u>

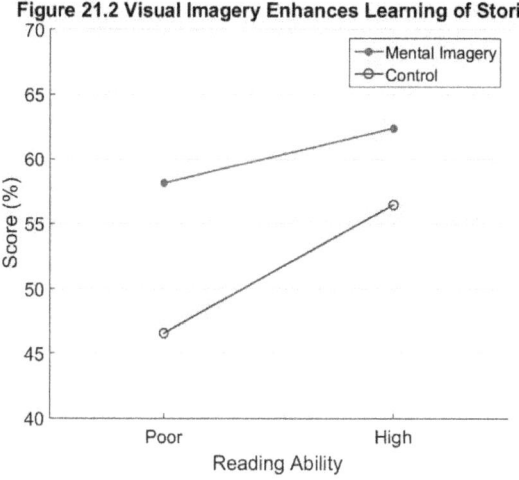

Figure 21.2 Visual Imagery Enhances Learning of Stories

For texts easy-to-imagine namely those supporting imaginal representations, visual imagery is a robust technique to enhance memory.

The keyword method

Richard Atkinson, the co-proposer of the process model of memory, created the "keyword method" for learning foreign languages. Two steps are involved in this method.

First, after seeing a foreign language word, pronounce it and think of a similar word in one's native language. Second, through visual imagination, establish a connection between the two words.

For instance, the Spanish word for duck is "pato," which is pronounced like "pot." One can imagine a duck running with a pot on his head without falling. The Spanish word for cow is "vaca," which pronounces like "vacuum" or "vacuum cleaner." So one may form an image of a cow working hard in the field with a vacuum cleaner on its head.

The effectiveness of the keyword method has been confirmed in the learning of Spanish, Russian, Chinese, Latin, etc. by English native speakers, in both adults and children.

In one study, Atkinson asked native English speakers to study 120 Russian words. Half of them used the keyword method, while the other half used rote learning. As shown in Figure 21.3, 5 days and 6 weeks after the initial learning, those using the keyword method could recall the meaning of more Russian words.

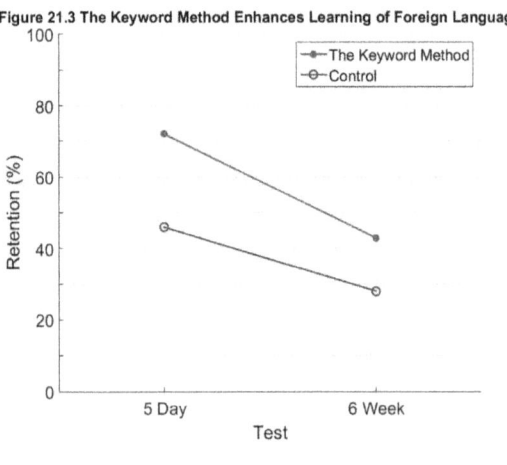

Figure 21.3 The Keyword Method Enhances Learning of Foreign Languages

Visual imagery for putting names to faces

There is a phenomenon called "Baker/baker Paradox." Psychologists show two people the same photo of a face and tell one of them this person is a baker and the other that his last name is Baker. Sometime later, when asked the initial word that paired with the photo, the person being told the last name is less likely to recall the paired word than the person given the profession.

Same photo, same word, but a different memory. Why?

<u>Professions are more meaningful than names and more easily linked to faces.</u>

<u>Names typically activate less semantic information compared to other meaningful information. Psychologists found that if we imagine people's names in a more meaningful way, our ability to remember names increases dramatically.</u>

One strategy is to use the keyword method introduced above. We first think of a homophonic word of people's name and then form a visual imagery of that word as it relates with the face (or some specific feature of the face) in meaningful and conceivable scenes.

Using this method, the American mnemonist Harry Lorayne claimed to be able to remember 400 names in 7 minutes in his *The Memory Book* (1974) co-authored with Jerry Lucas.

Confirming the effectiveness of this strategy, psychologists found that training people to use the keyword method almost doubled their ability to remember name-face pairs.

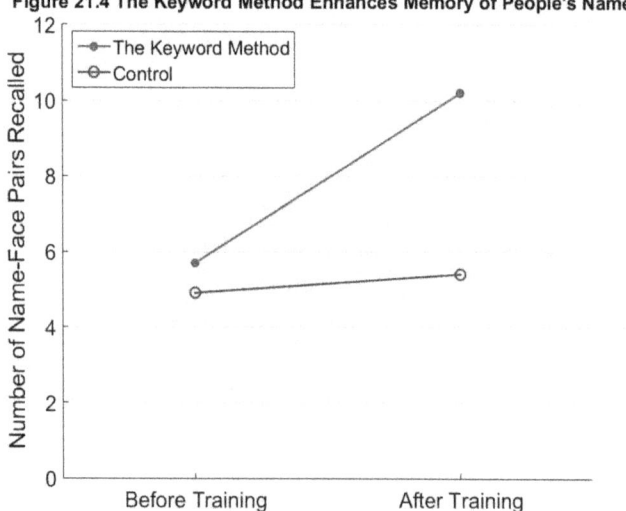

Figure 21.4 The Keyword Method Enhances Memory of People's Names

The Bizarreness Effect

<u>Perhaps the most effective way to form memorable mental images is in a bizarre manner. Bizarre or irrational information is more distinctive (Chapter 6) and attracts more attention.</u>

In daily life, we can create this Bizarreness Effect with three approaches: replacement, exaggeration, and activation.

To remember that you have locked the door, imagine using your head instead of the key to lock it. This is replacement.

To remember you put your glasses on the bed, imagine a giant version of your glasses is sleeping on your bed. This is exaggeration.

To remember to reply to someone's email, imagine the head of that person comes out of your computer and says "hello." This is activation or introducing actions.

CHAPTER 22
The Method of Loci

Eleanor A. Maguire, a neuroscientist at University College London, once studied 10 individuals with exceptional memories or memory masters—8 were World Memory Champions.

Through neuropsychological tests, Maguire found these memory masters were superior to the average person in terms of verbal working memory and verbal long-term memory. Yet, they were not different from the average person in general cognitive and reasoning ability such as IQ. Maguire scanned their brains using structural brain imaging techniques and found no difference with the brains of ordinary people.

Next, Maguire went on to see if the brains of the memory masters acted differently than the average person's. Maguire let everyone lie in a functional magnetic resonance imaging (fMRI) equipment and asked them to remember a variety of numbers, faces, and shapes of snowflakes.

As a result, the masters had surprisingly higher memory scores than the average person. Meanwhile, their medial superior parietal gyrus, retrosplenial cortex, and right posterior hippocampus were more active during the memory task. These brain regions are responsible for memory, especially spatial memory and navigation. Therefore, the masters might have used spatial strategies in memorizing the items.

This was confirmed when Maguire asked the masters to report their memory strategies. For instance, in the case of remembering numbers, the masters would first associate them with pictures of people, animals, or objects, and then put the pictures onto the sides of the road in their thinking space. To recall the numbers, they just walked along their thinking space and collected their memories.

This strategy of memory is "the method of loci." Loci is Latin for "places."

The method of loci explained

Around 500 B.C., when the Greek poet Simonides was reciting his poems to a large crowd at a banquet hall, he was called out to see two visitors. At the moment he stepped out of the hall, the hall collapsed, killing everyone inside. The victims were smashed and could not be recognized. Simonides was asked to help identify the victims for their respective families. To his surprise, he could recall all the names of the victims by referring to the seating arrangement.

This event inspired Simonides to develop a system of mnemonics based on images and places. This system is later known as "the method of loci" and the origin of mnemonics usually dates to this time. It is also called the journey, mental walk, or mind palace.

Later, the Roman philosopher Cicero explained the method in his *De oratore* like this:

"Persons desiring to train this faculty [of memory] must select places and form mental images of the things they wish to remember and store those images in the places, so that the order of the places will preserve the order of the things, and the images of the things will denote the things themselves."

Visual imagination is a powerful memory strategy, yet, it requires a memory clue to connect all the visual information in series. The method of loci serves this purpose and many professional mnemonists use it.

<u>If we link the items to be remembered with some specified locations, for instance, along familiar streets, when we want to retrieve the items, we just mentally walk through those locations.</u>

Now, think of 10 locations from your home to the nearest train or bus station. If that is difficult, change the station to a park or library.

The method of loci works for the average person as well

Two Italian psychologists, Rossana De Beni and Cesare Cornoldi, trained ordinary people to use the method of loci. They asked the subjects to think of 20 locations and then use these locations to memorize 20 triplets (groups of 3 nouns). Examples of the triplets included key-exhibition-fly, bone-picture-tomato, and car-canal-network.

The subjects were trained to form concrete visual images of the triplets and link the first noun of the triplets with the locations. For instance, in the example of the first triplets, if we use the entrance of a psychology department as the first location, we may think like this: when we open the door of the building with the key, we see an exhibition of fly samples from around the world.

People in the control group were asked to use this visual imagery strategy alone, knowing nothing about the method of loci. It was found that compared to subjects in the control group, those in the method of loci group remembered far more triplets.

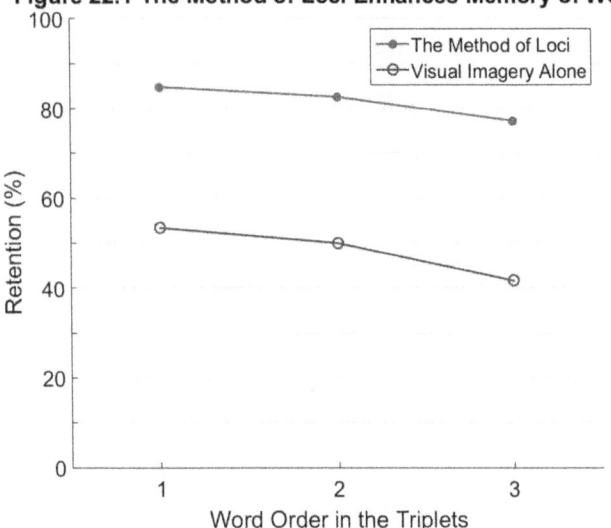

Figure 22.1 The Method of Loci Enhances Memory of Words

More familiar locations are preferred

Jessica Robin and Morris Moscovitch at the University of Toronto found that compared to less familiar locations, familiar locations enhance people's memory of information related to those locations.

They asked people to read texts about scenes and events associated with landmark buildings. During a later recall, it was found that people could recall scenes and events associated with familiar landmarks in more detail and at a faster speed.

Then Robin and Moscovitch asked people to imagine future events that were associated with the landmarks.

Similarly, when later asked to recall their imaginations, people told more details and did so at a faster speed when the imaginations were associated with familiar landmarks.

Street locations are better than room locations

German psychologist Cristina Massen at the Max Planck Institute for Human Cognitive and Brain Sciences asked college students and faculty members to practice the method of loci. Half of them used locations on their way from home to work/school. The other half used locations in their house from getting up to leaving home (like the kitchen and living room). They were then asked to memorize various word lists.

Those using street locations consistently outperformed those using home locations. This was true even for items related to streets (such as *ambulance*, *factory*, *police officer*) and houses (such as *coffee*, *meat*, *piano*). This is probably because the physical distance affects psychological distance so items stored farther away from each other can be better distinguished.

Chapter 23
The Peg-Word System

The peg-word system is another method that provides hooks for items to be remembered. In this system, numbers of 1–10 are retrieval cues, which are associated with items to be remembered through mediators easily visualized. The mediators are shown below, please take a minute or two to memorize them:

One is a gun/bun

Two is a shoe

Three is a tree

Four is a door

Five is a hive

Six is a stick

Seven is heaven

Eight is a gate

Nine is wine

Ten is a hen

As the next step, we just need to link information with the meditators in order.

The Peg-Word System

Practically, we can use the peg-word system to remember shopping lists, for instance. Please try to remember the following 10 nouns using the above system:

Apple, milk, clock, book, shirt, soap, tea, knife, scissor, pen

You can imagine:

"An apple sitting on a bun

A cup of milk standing on your shoes

A clock hanging on top of a tree

A door made of books

A shirt accidentally fell on the hive

You try to make fire by rubbing a stick with a soap"

And so on.

It is easy to form these mental images.

In one study, psychologists asked college students to memorize 7 word lists. Half of the students were told to use the peg-word system while the other half were only told to memorize the words without mentioning of any specific strategies. For a later test, recalling the right item at the right order was scored 2 points, while the right item at a wrong order 1.

As shown in Figure 23.1, it was found those using the peg-word system consistently outperformed the students in the control group.

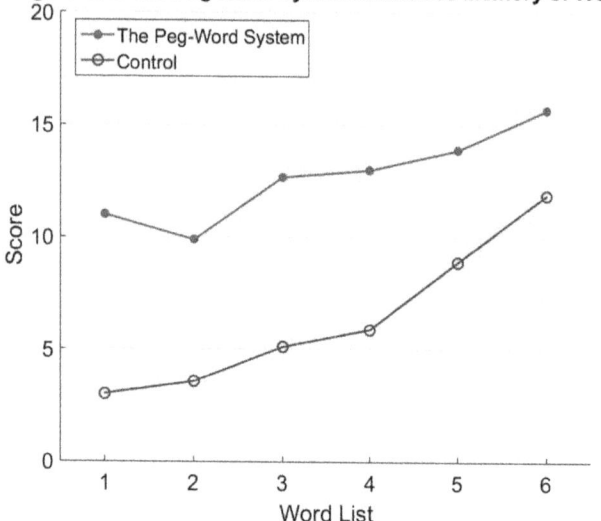

Figure 23.1 The Peg-Word System Enhances Memory of Words

Notably, the retroactive interference effect obvious in the students in the control group was substantially buffered in the students using the peg-word system.

Conclusions

We have gone on a journey across the natural history of learning and forgetting. Memory is encoded, stored, consolidated, retrieved, and reconsolidated. This gives us three time windows to interfere with memory: encoding, consolidation, and retrieval.

Encoding that attracts more attention and at a deeper level brings better memory. Encoding that activates prior knowledge and schemas will trigger a faster systems consolidation process and enhance memory. Repeated testing, especially when precise feedback is provided, is a more effective learning strategy than repeated studying.

To successfully retrieve a memory, any memory, creating (during encoding) and coming up with (at retrieval) effective cues is essential. You can use schematic, contextual, or mnemonic cues, depending on the learning materials and your preference.

You should combine different memory strategies and use them in a flexible way. For instance, you may use concept mapping as a testing tool to evaluate your learning.

Students with higher academic achievement have been reported to use a variety of effective strategies. In educational science, this is known as self-regulated learning. As the name reveals, self-regulated learning is a learning process during which students actively design and monitor their learning and use a variety of memory strategies.

In addition, along with the aging process, people's memory deteriorates. This has been linked to a reduced use of effective memory strategies in the aged. In a recent study, when instructed to use combined memory strategies, the memory performance of the elderly substantially increased. This evidence indicates the power of memory strategies.

In this book, we have presented many cognitive strategies towards superior memory. Now it is your turn to apply them in your everyday life. Best of luck!

References

Chapter 1

Ebbinghaus,H. (1964). *Über das Gedächtnis: Untersuchungen Zur Experimentellen Psychologie* [*Memory: A contribution to experimental psychology*] (H. A. Ruger & C. E. Bussenius, Trans.). New York: Dover. (Original work published 1885)

Slamecka, N. J. (1985). Ebbinghaus: Some associations. *Journal of Experimental Psychology: Learning, Memory, and Cognition*, 11,414-435.

Krueger, W. C. F. (1929). The effects of over- learning on retention. *Journal of Experimental Psychology*, 12, 71-78.

Thompson, C. P. (1982). Memory for unique personal events: The roommate study. *Memory & Cognition*, 10(4), 324-332.

Conway, M. A., Cohen, G., & Stanhope, N. (1991). On the very long-term retention of knowledge acquired through formal education: Twelve years of cognitive psychology. *Journal of Experimental Psychology: General*, 120(4), 395.

Bahrick, H. P. (1984). Semantic memory content in permastore: Fifty years of memory for Spanish learned in school. *Journal of experimental psychology: General*, 113(1), 1.

Chapter 2

Krueger, W. C. F. (1929). The effects of over- learning on retention. *Journal of Experimental Psychology*, 12, 71-78.

Driskell, J. E., Willis, R. P., & Copper, C. (1992). Effect of overlearning on retention. *Journal of Applied Psychology*, 77, 615-622.

Rohrer, D., Taylor, K., Pashler, H., Wixted, J. T., & Capeda, N. J. (2005). The effect of overlearning on long-term retention. *Applied Cognitive Psychology*, 19, 361-74.

Chapter 3

Jenkins, J. G., & Dallenbach, K. M. (1924). Obliviscence during sleep and waking. *The American Journal of Psychology*, 35(4), 605-612.

Hockey, G.R.J., Davies, S., 8c Gray, M.M. (1972). Forgetting as a function of sleep at different times of day. *Quarterly Journal of Experimental Psychology*, 24, 386-93.

Folkard, S., Monk, T. H., Bradbury, R., & Rosenthall, J. (1977). Time of day effects in school children's immediate and delayed recall of meaningful material. *British journal of Psychology*, 68(1), 45-50.

Chapter 4

Atkinson, R. C., & Shiffrin, R. M. (1968). Human memory: A proposed system and its control processes1. In *Psychology of learning and motivation* (Vol. 2, pp. 89-195). Academic Press.

Squire, L. R. (1992). Declarative and nondeclarative memory: Multiple brain systems supporting learning and memory. *Journal of cognitive neuroscience*, 4(3), 232-243.

References

Tulving, E. (1972). Episodic and semantic memory. In E. Tulving & W. Donaldson (Eds.), *Organization of Memory* (pp. 381-402). New York, NY: Academic Press.

Morris, R. G. M. (2006). Elements of a neurobiological theory of hippocampal function: the role of synaptic plasticity, synaptic tagging and schemas. *European Journal of Neuroscience*, 23(11), 2829-2846.

Wang, S. H., & Morris, R. G. (2010). Hippocampal-neocortical interactions in memory formation, consolidation, and reconsolidation. *Annual review of psychology*, 61, 49-79.

Dudai, Y., Karni, A., & Born, J. (2015). *The consolidation and transformation of memory*. Neuron, 88(1), 20-32.

Chapter 5

Wilson, M. A., & McNaughton, B. L. (1994). Reactivation of hippocampal ensemble memories during sleep. *Science*, 265(5172), 676-679.

Wang, S. H., & Morris, R. G. (2010). Hippocampal-neocortical interactions in memory formation, consolidation, and reconsolidation. *Annual review of psychology*, 61, 49-79.

Wagner, U., Gais, S., Haider, H., Verleger, R., & Born, J. (2004). Sleep inspires insight. *Nature*, 427(6972), 352.

Lahl, O., Wispel, C., Willigens, B., & Pietrowsky, R. (2008). An ultra short episode of sleep is sufficient to promote declarative memory performance. *Journal of sleep research*, 17(1), 3-10.

Lau, H., Alger, S. E., & Fishbein, W. (2011). Relational memory: a daytime nap facilitates the abstraction of general concepts. *PloS one*, 6(11), e27139.

Stickgold, R., James, L., & Hobson, J. A. (2000). Visual discrimination learning requires sleep after training. *Nature neuroscience*, 3(12), 1237.

Deary, I. J., & Tait, R. (1987). Effects of sleep disruption on cognitive performance and mood in medical house officers. *Br Med J (Clin Res Ed)*, 295(6612), 1513-1516.

Drummond, S. P., Brown, G. G., Gillin, J. C., Stricker, J. L., Wong, E. C., & Buxton, R. B. (2000). Altered brain response to verbal learning following sleep deprivation. *Nature*, 403(6770), 655.

Chapter 6

Martinussen, R., Hayden, J., Hogg-Johnson, S., & Tannock, R. (2005). A meta-analysis of working memory impairments in children with attention-deficit/hyperactivity disorder. *Journal of the American Academy of Child & Adolescent Psychiatry*, 44(4), 377-384.

Bradshaw, G. L., & Anderson, J. R. (1982). Elaborative encoding as an explanation of levels of processing. *Journal of Verbal Learning and Verbal Behavior*, 21, 165-74.

References

Craik, F. I., & Lockhart, R. S. (1972). Levels of processing: A framework for memory research. *Journal of verbal learning and verbal behavior*, 11(6), 671-684.

Crowder, R. G., & Morton, I. (1969). Precategorical acoustic storage (PAS). *Perception & Psychophysics*, 5, 365-373.

Schmidt, S. R. (1991). Can we have a distinctive theory of memory? *Memory and Cognition*, 19, 523-42.

Hunt, R. R., & Worthen, J. B. (Eds.). (2006) *Distinctiveness and memory*. Oxford, England: University Press

Fabiani, M., & Donchin, E. (1995). Encoding processes and memory organization: a model of the von Restorff effect. *Journal of Experimental Psychology: Learning, Memory, and Cognition*, 21(1), 224.

Watier, N., & Collin, C. (2012). The effects of distinctiveness on memory and metamemory for face–name associations. *Memory*, 20(1), 73-88.

Cashen, M. C., & Leicht, K. L. (1970). Role of the isolation effect in a formal educational setting. *Journal of Educational Psychology*, 61, 484-486.

Crouse, J. H., & Idstein, P. (1972). Effects of encoding cues on prose learning. *Journal of Educational Psychology*, 68, 309-313.

Rickards, J. P., & August G. J. (1975). Generative underlining strategies in prose recall. *Journal of Educational Psychology*, 67, 860-865.

Bell, K. E., & Limber, J. E. (2010). Reading skill, textbook marking, and course performance. *Literacy Research and Instruction*, 49, 56–67.

Chapter 7

Forrin, N. D., MacLeod, C. M., & Ozubko, J. D. (2012). Widening the boundaries of the production effect. *Memory & Cognition*, 40(7), 1046-1055.

Fawcett, J. M. (2013). The production effect benefits performance in between-subject designs: A meta-analysis. *Acta Psychologica*, 142(1), 1-5.

Wallace, W. T. (1994). Memory for music: Effect of melody on recall of text. *Journal of Experimental Psychology: Learning, Memory, and Cognition*, 20, 1471-1485.

Ludke, K. M., Ferreira, F., & Overy, K. (2014). Singing can facilitate foreign language learning. *Memory & cognition*, 42(1), 41-52.

Chapter 8

Brooks, L. (1967). The suppression of visualization by reading. *Quarterly Journal of Experimental Psychology*, 19, 289-299.

De Beni, R., & Moè, A. (2003). Presentation modality effects in studying passages. Are mental images always effective? *Applied Cognitive Psychology*, 17, 309-324.

Ginns, P. (2005). Meta-analysis of the modality effect. *Learning and instruction*, 15(4), 313-331.

References

Levin, J., & Divine-Hawkins, P. (1974). Visual imagery as a prose-learning process. *Journal of Reading Behavior*, 6, 23-30.

Mousavi, S.Y., Low, R. and Sweller, J. (1995). Reducing cognitive load by mixing auditory and visual presentation modes. *Journal of Educational Psychology*, 87(2) 319-334.

Mayer, R. E., & Moreno, R. (1998). A split-attention effect in multimedia learning: Evidence for dual processing systems in working memory. *Journal of educational psychology*, 90(2), 312.

Mayer, R. E. (2008). Applying the science of learning: Evidence-based principles for the design of multimedia instruction. *American psychologist*, 63(8), 760.

Chapter 9

Spilich, G. J., Vesonder, G. T., Chiesi, H. L., & Voss, J. F. (1979). Text processing of domain-related information for individuals with high and low domain knowledge. *Journal of verbal learning and verbal behavior*, 18(3), 275-290.

McNamara, D. S., & Kintsch, W. (1996). Learning from texts: Effects of prior knowledge and text coherence. *Discourse Processes*, 22, 247-288.

Shearer, B. A., Lundeberg, M. A., & Coballes-Vega, C. (1997). Making the connection between research and reality: Strategies teachers use to read and evaluate journal articles. *Journal of Educational Psychology*, 89, 592-598.

Topping, K. J., Samuels, J., & Paul, T. (2007). Does practice make perfect? Independent reading quantity, quality and student achievement. *Learning and Instruction*, 17(3), 253-264.

Chapter 10

Rumelhart, D. E. (1984). Schemata and the cognitive system. In R. S. Wyer & T. K. Srull, *Handbook of social cognition* (pp. 161–188). Hillsdale, NJ: Lawrence Erlbaum.

Bransford, J. D., & Johnson, M. K. (1972). Contextual prerequisites for understanding: Some investigations of comprehension and recall. *Journal of Verbal Learning and Verbal Behavior*, 11, 717-726.

Bradshaw, G. L., & Anderson, J. R. (1982). Elaborative encoding as an explanation of levels of processing. *Journal of Verbal Learning and Verbal Behavior*, 21, 165-74.

Gentner, D. (1989). analogical learning. *Similarity and analogical reasoning*, 199.

Gentner, D., & Gentner, D. R. (1983). Flowing waters or teeming crowds: Mental models of electricity. *Mental models*, 99-129.

Chapter 11

Ausubel, D.P. (2000). *The acquisition and retention of knowledge: a cognitive view*. Kluwer Academic Publishers.

References

Novak, J. D., & Musonda, D. (1991). A twelve-year longitudinal study of science concept learning. *American educational research journal*, 28(1), 117-153.

Hilbert, T. S., & Renkl, A. (2005, January). Individual Differences in Concept Mapping when Learning from Texts. In *Proceedings of the Annual Meeting of the Cognitive Science Society* (Vol. 27, No. 27).

Nesbit, J. C., & Adesope, O. O. (2006). Learning with concept and knowledge maps: A meta-analysis. *Review of educational research*, 76(3), 413-448.

Chapter 12

Bretzing, B. H., & Kulhavy, R. W. (1981). Note-taking and passage style. *Journal of Educational Psychology*, 73, 242-250.

Einstein, G. O., Morris, J., & Smith, S. (1985). Note-taking, individual differences, and memory for lecture information. *Journal of Educational Psychology*, 77, 522-532.

Van Meter, P. (2001). Drawing construction as a strategy for learning from text. *Journal of Educational Psychology*, 93, 129-140.

De Koning, B. B., & van der Schoot, M. (2013). Becoming part of the story! Refueling the interest in visualization strategies for reading comprehension. *Educational Psychology Review*, 25(2), 261-287.

Bretzing, B. H., & Kulhavy, R. W. (1979). Notetaking and depth of processing. *Contemporary Educational Psychology*, 4, 145-153.

Wittrock, M. C. (1990). Generative processes of comprehension. *Educational Psychologist*, 24, 345-376.

Pressley, M., McDaniel, M. A., Turnure, J. E., Wood, E., & Ahmad, M. (1987). Generation and precision of elaboration: Effects on intentional and incidental learning. *Journal of Experimental Psychology: Learning, Memory, and Cognition*, 13, 291-300.

Rawson, K. A., & Van Overschelde, J. P. (2008). How does knowledge promote memory? The distinctiveness theory of skilled memory. *Journal of Memory and Language*, 58, 646-668.

Furtak, E. M., Seidel, T., Iverson, H., & Briggs, D. C. (2012). Experimental and quasi-experimental studies of inquiry-based science teaching: A meta-analysis. *Review of Educational Research*, 82(3), 300-329.

Chapter 13

Ballard, P. B. (1913). Obliviscence and Reminiscence. *British Journal of Psychology*.

Roediger III, H. L., & Karpicke, J. D. (2006). Test-enhanced learning: Taking memory tests improves long-term retention. *Psychological science*, 17(3), 249-255.

References

Karpicke, J. D., & Roediger, H. L. (2008). The critical importance of retrieval for learning. *Science*, 319(5865), 966-968.

Carpenter, S. K., & DeLosh, E. L. (2006). Impoverished cue support enhances subsequent retention: Support for the elaborative retrieval explanation of the testing effect. *Memory & cognition*, 34(2), 268-276.

Zaromb, F. M., & Roediger, H. L. (2010). The testing effect in free recall is associated with enhanced organizational processes. *Memory & Cognition*, 38(8), 995-1008.

Rawson, K. A., Dunlosky, J., & Sciartelli, S. M. (2013). The power of successive relearning: Improving performance on course exams and long-term retention. *Educational Psychology Review*, 25(4), 523-548.

Pyc, M. A., & Rawson, K. A. (2011). Costs and benefits of dropout schedules of test-restudy practice: Implications for student learning. *Applied Cognitive Psychology*, 25, 87-95.

Karpicke, J.D., and Roediger, H.L., III (2008). The Critical Importance of Retrieval for Learning. *Science*, 319, 966-968.

Chapter 14

Raaijmakers, J.G.W. & Shiffrin, R.M. (1980). SAM: A theory of probabilistic search in associative memory. In G.H. Bower (Ed.), *The psychology of learning and motivation: Advances in research and theory*. Vol. 14 (Pp. 207-262). New York: Academic Press

Raaijmakers, J. G. W., & Shiffrin, R. M. (1981). Search of associative memory. *Psychological Review*, 88, 93-134

Raaijmakers, J. G. W. (2003). Spacing and repetition effects in human memory: application of the SAM model. *Cognitive Science*, 27, 431-52

Shiffrin, R. M., & Steyvers, M. (1997). A model for recognition memory: REM—retrieving effectively from memory. *Psychonomic bulletin & review*, 4(2), 145-166.

Mueller, S. T., & Shiffrin, R. M. (2006, June). REM II: A model of the developmental co-evolution of episodic memory and semantic knowledge. In *International conference on learning and development (ICDL)*, Bloomington, IN.

Davelaar, E.J., & Raaijmakers, J.G.W. (2012). Human memory search. In *Cognitive Search: Evolution, Algorithms, and the Brain*. Strüngmann Forum Report, vol. 9, J. Lupp, series ed. (Pp. 177-193). Cambridge, MA: MIT Press.

Tulving, E., & Thomson, D. M. (1973). Encoding specificity and retrieval processes in episodic memory. *Psychological Review*, 80, 359-380.

Davis, R. L., & Zhong, Y. (2017). The biology of forgetting—a perspective. *Neuron*, 95(3), 490-503.

Wagenaar, W. A. (1986). My memory: A study of autobiographical memory over six years. *Cognitive Psychology*, 18, 225-252.

References

Mäantylä, T. (1986). Optimizing cue effectiveness: Recall of 500 and 600 incidentally learned words. *Journal of Experimental Psychology: Learning, Memory, and Cognition*, 12(1), 66.

Chapter 15

Chinese language story, cited in Spear, N. E., & Riccio, D. C. (1994). *Memory: Phenomena and principles*. Allyn & Bacon. p53-54.

Godden, D. R., & Baddeley, A. D. (1975). Context-dependent memory in two natural environments: On land and underwater. *British Journal of psychology*, 66(3), 325-331.

Godden, D., & Baddeley, A. (1980). When does context influence recognition memory?. *British journal of Psychology*, 71(1), 99-104.

Smith, S. M. (1985). Background music and context-dependent memory. *American Journal of Psychology*, 98, 591-603

Goodwin, D. W., Powell, B., Bremer, D., Hoine, H., & Stern, J. (1969). Alcohol and recall: State dependent effects in man. *Science*, 163, 1358-1360.

Eich, J. E. (1980). The cue-dependent nature of state-dependent retrieval. *Memory & Cognition*, 8. 157-173.

actors remember scripts… see discussion in Foer, J. (2012). *Moonwalking with Einstein: The art and science of remembering everything*. Penguin.

Smith, S. M. & Vela, E. (2001). Environmental context-dependent memory: A Review and meta-analysis. *Psychonomic Bulletin & Review*, 8, 203-220.

Smith, S.M. (1984). A comparison of two techniques for reducing context-dependent forgetting. *Memory & Cognition*, 12, 477-482.

Smith, S. M., Glenberg, A., & Bjork, R. A. (1978). Environmental context and human memory. *Memory & Cognition*, 6(4), 342-353.

Smith, S. M. (2007). Context and human memory. In H. L. Roediger, III, Y. Dudai, and S. M. Fitzpatrick (Eds.) *Science of Memory: Concepts*, Oxford University Press, pp. 111-114.

Chapter 16

Bahrick, H. P., Bahrick, L. E., Bahrick, A. S., & Bahrick, P. E. (1993). Maintenance of foreign language vocabulary and the spacing effect. *Psychological Science*, 4(5), 316-321.

Sobel, H. S., Cepeda, N. J., & Kapler, I. V. (2011). Spacing effects in real-world classroom vocabulary learning. *Applied Cognitive Psychology*, 25, 763-767.

Cepeda, N. J., Pashler, H., Vul, E., Wixted, J. T., & Rohrer, D. (2006). Distributed practice in verbal recall tasks: A review and quantitative synthesis. *Psychological bulletin*, 132(3), 354.

References

Cepeda, N. J., Vul, E., Rohrer, D., Wixted, J. T., & Pashler, H. (2008). Spacing effects in learning: A temporal ridgeline of optimal retention. *Psychological science*, 19(11), 1095-1102.

Fixed vs extended spacing... Carpenter, S. K., Cepeda, N. J., Rohrer, D., Kang, S. H., & Pashler, H. (2012). Using spacing to enhance diverse forms of learning: Review of recent research and implications for instruction. *Educational Psychology Review*, 24(3), 369-378.

Glenberg, Arthur M. (1979), Component-Levels Theory of the. Effects of Spacing of Repetitions on Recall and Recognition. *Memory and cognition*, 7, 2, 95-112.

Greene, R. L. (1989). Spacing effects in memory: Evidence for a two-process account. *Journal of Experimental Psychology: Learning, Memory, and Cognition*, 15, 371-377.

Chapter 17

Rohrer, D., & Taylor, K. (2007). The shuffling of mathematics problems improves learning. *Instructional Science*, 35, 481–498.

Kornell, N., & Bjork, R. A. (2008). Learning concepts and categories: Is spacing the "enemy of induction"?. *Psychological science*, 19(6), 585-592.

Hatala, R. M., Brooks, L. R., & Norman, G. R. (2003). Practice makes perfect: the critical role of mixed practice in the acquisition of ECG interpretation skills. *Advances in Health Sciences Education*, 8(1), 17-26.

Taylor, K., & Rohrer, D. (2010). The effects of interleaved practice. *Applied Cognitive Psychology*, 24, 837–848.

Chapter 18

Anderson, M. C. (2003). Rethinking interference theory: Executive control and the mechanisms of forgetting. *Journal of Memory and Language*, 49, 415-445.

Jonides, J., Lewis, R. L., Nee, D. E., Lustig, C. A., Berman, M. G., & Moore, K. S. (2008). The mind and brain of short-term memory. *Annu. Rev. Psychol.*, 59, 193-224.

McGeoch, J.A. and McDonald, W.T. (1931) Meaningful relation and retroactive inhibition, *American Journal of Psychology* 43:579–88

Crouse, J. H. (1971). Retroactive interference in reading prose materials. *Journal of Educational Psychology*, 62(1), 39.

Tulving, E. and Psotka, J. (1971) Retroactive inhibition in free recall: Inaccessibility of information available in the memory store. *Journal of Experimental psychology*, 87, 1-8

Bäuml, K.-H. T. & Kliegl, O. (2013). The critical role of retrieval processes in release from proactive interference. *Journal of Memory and Language*, 68, 39-53.

Gunter, B., Berry, C., & Clifford, B. (1981). Proactive interference effects with television news items: Further evidence. *Journal of Experimental Psychology: Human Learning & Memory*, 7 (6), 480-487.

References

Wickens, D. D. (1970). Encoding categories of words: An empirical approach to meaning. *Psychological Review*, 77, 1-15.

Wissman, K. T., Rawson, K. A., & Pyc, M. A. (2011). The interim test effect: Testing prior material can facilitate the learning of new material. *Psychonomic Bulletin & Review*, 18(6), 1140-1147.

Potts, R., & Shanks, D. R. (2012). Can testing immunize memories against interference?. *Journal of Experimental Psychology: Learning, Memory, and Cognition*, 38(6), 1780.

Chapter 19

F.C. Bartlett (1932). *Remembering: a study in experimental and social psychology*. London: Cambridge University Press.

Hastorf, A., & Cantril, H. (1954). They saw a game: A case study. *Journal of Abnormal Psychology,* 49, 129-134.

Anderson, R. C., & Pichert, J. W. (1978). Recall of previously unrecallable information following a shift in perspective. *Journal of verbal learning and verbal behavior*, 17(1), 1-12.

Roediger, H. L., & McDermott, K. B. (1995). Creating false memories: Remembering words not presented in lists. *Journal of experimental psychology: Learning, Memory, and Cognition*, 21(4), 803.

Bransford, J.D., Barclay, J.R. and Franks, J.J. (1972) Sentence memory: a constructive versus interpretative approach. *Cognitive Psychology* 3: 193-209.

Owens, J., Bower, G. H., & Black, J. B. (1979). The "soap opera" effect in story recall. *Memory & Cognition*, 7(3), 185-191.

Chapter 20

Yates, F. A. (1966). *The art of memory*. University of Chicago Press.

Foer, J. (2012). *Moonwalking with Einstein: The art and science of remembering everything*. Penguin.

Chapter 21

Shepard, R. N. (1967). Recognition memory for words, sentences, and pictures. *journal of Verbal Learning and Verbal Behavior*, 6, 156-163.

Paivio, A. (1971). *Imagery and verbal processes*. London, England: Holt, Rinehart & Winston.

Paivio, A. (1976). Imagery in recall and recognition. In J.Brown (Ed.), *Recall and recognition* (pp. 103– 129). New York, NY: Wiley.

Snodgrass, J. G., Wasser, B., Finkelstein, M., & Goldberg, L. B. (1974). On the fate of visual and verbal memory codes for pictures and words: Evidence for a dual coding mechanism in recognition memory. *Journal of Verbal Learning and Verbal Behavior*, 13, 27– 37

Nelson, D. L. (1979). Remembering pictures and words: Appearance, significance, and name. In L. S.Cermak & F. I.

References

M.Craik (Eds.), *Levels of processing in human memory* (pp. 45– 76). Hillsdale, NJ: Erlbaum

Nelson, D. L., Reed, V. S., & Walling, J. R. (1976). Pictorial superiority effect. *Journal of Experimental Psychology: Human Learning and Memory*, 2, 523– 528.

Grady, C. L., McIntosh, A. R., Rajah, M. N., & Craik, F. I. (1998). Neural correlates of the episodic encoding of pictures and words. *Proceedings of the National Academy of Sciences*, 95(5), 2703-2708.

Bower, G. H. (1970). Imagery as a relational organizer in associative learning. *Journal of Verbal Learning and Verbal Behavior*, 9, 529-533.

Bower, G.H. (1972). Mental imagery and associative learning. In L. Gregg (Ed.), *Cognition in Learning and Memory*, 51-88.

Pressley, G.M. (1976) Mental imagery helps eight-year-olds remember what they read. *Journal of Educational Psychology*, 68: 355-9

Atkinson, R. C. (1975). Mnemotechnics in second-language learning. *American Psychologist*, 30, 821-828.

Beaton, A., Gruneberg, M., Hyde, C., Shufflebottom, A., & Sykes, R. (2005). Facilitation of receptive and productive foreign vocabulary learning using the keyword method: The role of image quality. *Memory*, 13(5), 458-471.

Pressley, M. (1977). Children's use of the keyword method to learn simple Spanish vocabulary words. *Journal of Educational Psychology*, 69(5), 465–472

Pressley, M., Levin, J. R., Nakamura, G. V., Hope, D. J., Bispo, J. G., & Toye, A. R. (1980). The keyword method of foreign vocabulary learning: An investigation of its generalizability. *Journal of Applied Psychology*, 65(6), 635.

Cohen, G. (1990). Why is it difficult to put names to faces? *British Journal of Psychology*. 81. 287-298.

Morris, P.E., Jones, S., & Hampson, P. (1978). An imagery mnemonic for the learning of people's names. *British Journal of Psychology*. 69, 335-336.

Davidson, D., Larson, S., Luo, Z., & Burden, M. (2000). Interruption and bizarreness effects in the recall of script-based text. *Memory*, 8 (4), 217-. 234.

Chapter 22

Yates, F. A. (1966). *The art of memory*. University of Chicago Press.

Foer, J. (2012). *Moonwalking with Einstein: The art and science of remembering everything*. Penguin.

Maguire, E. A., Valentine, E. R., Wilding, J. M., & Kapur, N. (2003). Routes to remembering: the brains behind superior memory. *Nature neuroscience*, 6(1), 90.

References

Bower, G. H. (1970). Analysis of a mnemonic device: Modern psychology uncovers the powerful components of an ancient system for improving memory. *American Scientist*, 58(5), 496-510.

De Beni, R., & Cornoldi, C. (1985). Effects of the mnemotechnique of loci in the memorization of concrete words. *Acta Psychologica*, 60, 11-24.

Robin, J., & Moscovitch, M. (2014). The effects of spatial contextual familiarity on remembered scenes, episodic memories, and imagined future events. *Journal of Experimental Psychology: Learning, Memory, and Cognition*, 40(2), 459.

Massen, C., Vaterrodt-Plünnecke, B., Krings, L., & Hilbig, B. E. (2009). Effects of instruction on learners' ability to generate an effective pathway in the method of loci. *Memory*, 17(7), 724-731.

Chapter 23

Bugelski, B. R. (1968). Images as mediators in one-trial paired-associate learning: II. Self-timing in successive lists. *Journal of Experimental Psychology*, 77(2), 328.

Conclusions

Hay, D. B. (2007). Using concept maps to measure deep, surface and non-learning outcomes. *Studies in Higher Education*, 32(1), 39-57.

Bednall, T. C., & Kehoe, E. J. (2011). Effects of self-regulatory instructional aids on self-directed study. *Instructional Science*, 39(2), 205-226.

Hinault, T., Lemaire, P., & Touron, D. (2017). Strategy combination during execution of memory strategies in young and older adults. *Memory*, 25(5), 619-625.

Index

abstraction, 36, 38, 39, 40, 41, 43

advance organizer, 85, 87, 90

afternoon, 27, 28

analogy, 82

assimilation, 36, 38, 39, 40, 84, 85

Assimilation Theory, 84, 85, 87

attention, 39, 50, 53, 54, 55, 63, 129, 163, 173

auditory, 31, 52, 53, 59, 63, 67, 140

blocked learning, 130, 131

chunking, 82, 83

concept map, 87, 88, 89, 90, 173, → mind map

consolidation, 25, 35, 36, 37, 38, 39, 40, 41, 43, 44, 45, 48, 70, 74, 77, 80, 82, 84, 90, 96, 102, 128, 129, 134, 144, 158, 173

context, 33, 36, 40, 65, 79, 80, 82, 85, 109, 114, 117, 118, 119, 120, 129, 173

creativity, 3

daytime, 24, 25, 39, 40

distinctive, 54, 55, 163

Distinctiveness Effect, 54, 157

Ebbinghaus, 6, 7, 9, 17, 23, 24

episodic, 33, 35, 36, 38, 52, 109

feedback, 99, 100, 101, 102, 103, 104, 106, 173

forgetting curve, 8, 9, 11, 12, 13, 18, 23, 112, 121, 156

Frederick C. Bartlett, 77, 143

free recall, 10, 25, 41, 60, 90, 92, 99, 101, 110, 122, 137, 141

hierarchical, 84, 87, 91

Hippocampal-Neocortical Interactions Theory, 34

hippocampus, 35, 36, 38, 39, 40, 46, 70, 165

insight, 3, 31, 40, 41, 42

interleaved learning, 130, 140

language, 12, 54, 60, 62, 70, 71, 114, 121, 159

Levels of Processing, 52, 54

massed learning, 119, 122, 128, 130

meaningful, 2, 10, 12, 84, 85, 118, 152, 153, 161

memory strength, 109, 118

meta-analysis, 20, 89

mind map, 87

Modality Effect, 63, 64, 157

morning, 25, 26, 27, 28, 29, 147

Mozart, 115

neocortex, 35, 36, 38, 40, 46, 70

Newton, 80, 81

nighttime, 24, 25

nonsense syllables, 7, 9, 17, 24

overlearning, 18, 19, 20, 21, 22, → rote learning

proactive interference, 134, 135, 139, 140, 141, 142

Production Effect, 58

psychophysics, 6

reading ability, 57, 70, 71, 75, 76, 158

recognition, 12, 13, 14, 15, 41, 58, 110, 122, 156

reminiscence, 98

retroactive interference, 135, 137, 138, 142, 172

Richard Atkinson, 30, 159

Index

rote learning, 18, 19, 22, 84, 160

schema, 36, 54, 74, 77, 79, 82, 85, 90, 96, 118, 143, 144, 145, 146, 147, 173

semantic, 33, 36, 38, 42, 51, 52, 53, 54, 57, 90, 96, 118, 129, 157, 161

sensory, 31, 35, 50, 52, 157

short-term memory, 31, 38, 46, 50, 53

spaced learning, 122, 126, 128, 129, 130, 134

Spanish, 13, 14, 121, 122, 159, 160

Swahili, 106, 142

visual, 31, 39, 44, 51, 52, 53, 63, 64, 91, 140, 152, 153, 156, 157, 158, 159, 161, 166, 167, 170

working memory, 31, 50, 63, 164

About The Author

Dr. Chong Chen is a neuroscientist and possesses a Ph.D. in Medicine. Chong has authored 10 books, including two series called *The Anchor of Our Purest Thoughts* and *Your Baby's Developing Brain*.

As far as the future goes, Chong hopes that he will be able to translate scientific findings into ways that will allow regular people to live better lives. And through his books, he hopes that he can reach a much wider audience.

You can contact Chong and follow what he is writing about at: https://brainandlife.net.

www.ingramcontent.com/pod-product-compliance
Lightning Source LLC
Chambersburg PA
CBHW051754040426
42446CB00007B/358